DRINKING CAMEL'S MILK IN THE YURT

EXPAT STORIES FROM KAZAKHSTAN

Edited by Monica Neboli

First published Great Britain 2013
by Summertime Publishing

ISBN 978-1-909193-23-9

Design by Creation Booth (www.creationbooth.com)
Cover photo: Eleonora Le Rose

For my daughters, Eleonora and Agata

Contents

Acknowledgements

This project began in 2011, while I was living in Kazakhstan, and has lasted almost two years. During this time a lot happened, including the return to my home country, Italy. This, as you can imagine, brought not just reverse culture shock, but also several changes in my life, all of which led to a significant slowdown of the initiative. Without the help of some precious travel companions, I would have struggled to get to the end at all.

Among those to whom I owe much are three friends who, to a varying degree but with equal enthusiasm, accompanied and supported me during the creation of this anthology. These are also people with whom I shared my expat experience in Kazakhstan... Sholpan Iskendirova for helping me to look beyond appearances and stereotypes and for showing me the extraordinary and fascinating culture of her country; Arianna Gianola for supporting the idea and for invaluable marketing efforts during the initial writers' competition – not to mention her advice, suggestions and encouragement along the way; my dear Annemarie van Klooster, with whom I spent evenings working on the project, all the way from the website construction to the final draft of the anthology. I thank her for being constantly available and for her commitment and professional contributions to the book.

To Jo Parfitt of Summertime Publishing, who believed in the project and has made it possible, and to Renata Harper who gave form to this anthology.

To the Embassy of Kazakhstan in Italy – in particular Ambassador Adrian Yelemessov, Prime Secretary Aigul Bokaeva and Honorary Consul Pierluigi Aluisio – for their patronage and for recognising the value of this anthology in contributing to a better understanding of the Kazakh culture among the expat community.

To Francesco, my lifelong partner, for standing beside me throughout the process. He has been my inspiration and motivation for continuing to be focused on my passions. I also thank my wonderful daughters, Eleonora and Agata, for being so understanding on those weekends when I was working on the book instead of playing games with them. I'd also like to thank my parents and the rest of my family for having promoted the final product beyond all expectations.

My final thanks to all the special fellow expats and travellers who, moved by the common desire of sharing the unforgettable experiences they have lived in this magical country, have made this anthology possible.

Foreword

You are about to read a collection of short stories about my country, the Republic of Kazakhstan. This book describes Kazakhstan through the eyes of foreigners, ordinary people who, by fate – or rather, by fortune – came to work and live in this beautiful country. As Ambassador of the Republic of Kazakhstan to Italy, but first and foremost as a Kazakh citizen, I am filled with pride and joy – pride for my homeland; joy because this book will introduce readers to Kazakhstan and its residents, traditions and culture.

While reading this anthology, you will pass through some of Kazakhstan's cities (perhaps unknown to you before); you will become acquainted with the country's hospitable and friendly people; you will come to know more about local cuisine and crafts. And all this, I hope, will create a better understanding of us, the people of Kazakhstan, and perhaps shatter some stereotypes too. If you want to draw your own conclusions about this country, read these stories, for you will find in them dialogues with ordinary locals and a description of their life and manners, as well as the authors' reflections on historical and contemporary Kazakhstan.

Why are these stories so interesting? Because all are firsthand, real and original!

Come to Kazakhstan: we welcome you as our guests. Don't be surprised if a stranger pays for your taxi or takes your hand and helps you cross the road. Or if, on asking someone for directions to your hotel, he invites you to his house to meet his family and treats you to a tasty dinner. When the time comes to say goodbye, the family may offer you simple gifts, with such open hearts and kind words that you might burst into tears.

Enjoy the simple human values of the Kazakh people, their friendship, love, hospitality, trust and honesty... and share your experiences with your family and friends on returning home.

I want to thank everyone who contributed to this book, who shared with us, their readers, all these unforgettable experiences – sometimes touching, sometimes funny – of travelling to a distant and unknown country.

Enjoy your reading!

Andrian Yelemessov, Ambassador of the
Republic of Kazakhstan to Italy

Introduction

One cold yet sunny afternoon in March 2011, there was a knock at the door of our house in Atyrau. A small middle-aged man of composed manner followed me into the living room, an amused smile on his face.

My family and I had been in Kazakhstan for two years and I had decided to organise a series of seminars for the expatriate community in Atyrau. The seminars, entitled 'Fundamentals of living in Kazakhstan', were intended as a forum to discuss the process of adjusting to our host country, as well as to introduce expatriates to the history, culture and traditions of Kazakhstan. We were also to discuss culture shock and other topics with which most, if not all, expats eventually become familiar.

To make the seminars a success however, I needed help. I needed the insights of someone deeply familiar with the country. And this is why Kuttygul Zambirbaev had arrived on my doorstep. A Kazakh friend had suggested Kuttygul as a co-host of the seminars and had set up this introduction. Kuttygul, a history teacher at a local secondary school, was delighted that members of the international community in this small city were interested in his country and he agreed, with much enthusiasm, to collaborate on the project.

I was enraptured by the proud voice of this petite man sitting upright before me in my living room. During his quietly delivered, but intense, two-hour narration, fascinating scenes of Kazakstan's history passed before my eyes, from the tribalism of the Hordes to the Kazakh Khanate, from Russian influence to independence. Kuttygul's pride in his country was a characteristic that I had come to recognise in the Kazakhs, particularly in the older generation. I had also come to appreciate the deep connection many Kazakhs have with nature and its elements. This struck me as deeply romantic and in many ways reminded me of the native American Indians, a sentiment that accompanied me throughout my years in Kazakhstan. (Indeed, once back in my home country a few years later, I read in *National Geographic* that anthropologists had discovered a genetic connection between the two groups; this did not take me by surprise. According to the scholars, thousands of years ago Asians from the Altai Mountains, the mountains on the border between China, Kazakhstan and Mongolia, crossed the piece of land which is now the Bering Strait into North America.)

After that afternoon with Kuttygul, I was inspired to do more to bring this country to the attention of newly arrived expats as well as those who, like myself before I had moved there, could not locate it on a map. I wanted to collect the experiences of the many expatriates who had been charmed by this country; to hear the stories of those who, in their own way, had been enriched by their experiences of the country, whether through its people, its values or its endless landscape.

One's first experience with Kazakhstan is not always easy; we need the right eyes to understand and appreciate what we see. The severity of the climate, the apparent coldness of the people, the long distances, the vast and largely still wild land... these are elements that can test the expatriate. But if we dig beyond the surface, we can soon discover that those elements that at first seemed adverse in fact represent the strengths of a country. Suddenly new horizons are opened up to the expat.

I remember well my family's first flight into Atyrau from Cairo. While descending, my eldest daughter, Eleonora, who was two and a half years old at the time, and I looked out the window of the plane, only to come to the conclusion that we were landing in the middle of nowhere.

"Mom, but where is the city?" she asked me, all innocence. "There's nothing below us!"

The scattering of houses, that from the plane seemed little more than a village in the middle of the steppe, were to become our world for the next two years. Discovering Kazakhstan was, for me, a conquest, and like all things that must be conquered, it took time, curiosity and a certain spirit of adventure.

Drinking Camel's Milk in the Yurt is a window into Kazakhstan and beyond. This anthology is a collection of expatriate experiences that have taken place all around the country, from its most desolate areas to its most modern cities. The stories have been shared by those who have experienced the difficulties of this land but did not let that stop them. Their enquiring minds have enabled them to discover the true charm of Kazakhstan; the sounds, scents, tastes and emotions that make up this incredible land and its people, the 'sons of the Steppe'.

As one of our authors writes, this is a land "driven by the memory of a nomadic world and its rules of hospitality, a world in which complete strangers have to care for each other under the most adverse of circumstances".

I hope that in reading *Drinking Camel's Milk in the Yurt* you are inspired to visit Kazakhstan and to explore it in the spirit of these stories. For if you do, I am sure this land will too have you spellbound...

Monica Neboli, July 2013

4

Chapter 1

The Arrival

First Snow

by Jacyntha England

As the plane begins its final descent into Almaty, the passengers prepare for landing by pulling winter clothes out of their carry-on bags. Bronzed shoulders are suddenly wrapped in wool pashminas or thick knitted sweaters, while neatly pedicured toes are shoved into layers of heavy socks, and tight-fitting boots. Children who have spent the past week playing on the beaches of southern Thailand, whine as their grandmothers force gloves and hats onto sunburned skin, and tighten scarves around wailing throats. By the time the plane lands, not a trace remains of the endless summer we left behind in Bangkok, a mere seven hours ago. In just a few minutes, all the passengers on board Air Astana flight 782 have transformed from carefree vacationers into hardened winter travelers.

All the passengers, that is, except me. New to Kazakhstan and its winters, I stand out like a sore thumb amongst my fellow travelers, for I have not thought to bring any warm clothing on this flight. I left Almaty two weeks ago, when the Tien Shan mountains stood bare against the blazing blue sky each morning and the sun still shone brightly each afternoon. As I packed my backpack on that sunny day in early October, I could focus only on my own exhaustion and need for a break from the culture shock that had been my constant companion since arriving in the country in August. That morning, I was running away; away from my loneliness and isolation as a newcomer to a city and people that seemed so closed and distant, away from a job that only managed to frustrate and disappoint me, away from food that made me feel queasy and bloated, and words that got caught in my throat just when I needed them most. I had come very close to giving up and leaving Kazakhstan many times since arriving, and the thought of returning to Almaty after my holiday had been just one dark day in a dim and distant future.

But now that day is here. Two weeks on a beach have left me feeling human again, and I have been flying over the mountains and deserts of Central Asia determined to make a fresh start. My backpack is full of scarves, perfumes and incense sticks that I plan to give to my Kazakh neighbors and colleagues, and crammed into my carry-on bag are curry sauces, bootleg DVDs and trashy paperbacks; small personal treats bought on impulse in Bangkok's Khaosan Road. With my rosy new attitude, it had not occurred to me that, somehow, I might be landing in Almaty in the dead of night – and one of the coldest nights of the year, too.

The airport doors slide open and the first blast of Kazakh winter almost knocks me to my knees. The pavement is slippery against my useless tropical flip-flops, and within seconds my toes have begun to go numb. Groups of returning Kazakh nationals rush past me, hugging and kissing relatives who have braved the weather this late at night to come and greet them, exchanging words that I can only guess are full of love and celebration. I stand and wait, digging around in my purse for leftover tenge, and trying to remember the right words to use when negotiating a taxi into town, feeling more alone than I have in years. Whatever strength I thought I had gained on the holiday seems to be fading into oblivion, as the cold keeps biting into my skin and eyes, making every bone in my body ache.

Suddenly, I feel a warm hand on mine. I instinctively recoil to this strange touch, and my eyes meet a pair of soft brown eyes nestled in the weathered and wrinkled face of an old man. He is reaching for my backpack, trying to help me carry it.

"Taxi, *devushka*?" he asks in a gentle voice.

I nod, and hold up five fingers to show how much I am willing to pay.

The man smiles, picks up my backpack and begins walking. I follow him, keeping my arms wrapped around my chest for warmth, and trying not to fall on the ice. When we get to his car, a rusty old four-seater, I immediately begin to open the back door, but he shakes his head and gestures to the front. I sit down next to him and close my eyes, the exhaustion from the trip and return to Almaty overwhelming me. As I begin to drift off, I can hear the old man muttering, "*holodno*", the Russian word for cold, as he starts the engine.

I must have fallen asleep for just a few seconds, for when I wake up the car engine is running and we have not yet left the parking lot. I can feel a blanket being wrapped around my shoulders, and glance up to see the old man squatting on the pavement beside the passenger seat, tucking the blanket along the side of my body.

When he sees I am awake, he smiles and winks.

"*Vsyo normalno devushka, seichas ne holodno,*" he says.

My Russian is still so rudimentary that I don't understand much beyond *normalno* [fine, or okay], but I know he is trying to make me more comfortable for the journey. In most other parts of the world, I would never let a male stranger so close to me, but somehow I feel I can trust this old man with his kind eyes and gentle voice.

He is singing now, a soft lullaby in Kazakh, as he tucks the blanket around my bare feet. He reaches into the back seat and pulls out a dented tin thermos. When he opens the lid, the scent of fresh tea with milk fills the space between us. He pours the hot liquid into a cup and passes it to me; I hold the cup between my hands and let it warm my chilled fingers. We stay like this, me holding the cup of tea and snug under the blankets, and him singing softly in the language of his ancestors, for most of the drive into the city. I slowly begin to relax as we pass the milestones of the highway, the factories and car showrooms illuminated under flickering streetlights.

Just as we reach the Central Mosque, with its towering blue minarets, the faintest drops of white start hitting the car's windshield.

"Ah," says my companion, a grin of delight spreading across his face and softening his wrinkles, "*pervy sneg.*" ["First snow."]

I will learn later that this evening has brought the first snowfall of the year, a sign of the changing seasons in a land that still abides by nature's laws. For now, however, I am content to burrow deeper under the blankets and watch the snow fall gently across the tips of the trees that line Almaty's main boulevards. We pass the cathedral, its golden onion-shaped domes glittering under the moonlight, then the grand tsarist mansions and Soviet statues of the main square, and finally the blue and white cottages that line the small canal that signals our entry to my neighborhood. Some of these buildings have been here for centuries, and at this time of night, as our lone car moves across a thin layer of pure, fresh snow, there is an inescapable sense of magic to our journey; as if we are being accompanied by generations of previous winter travelers across a timeless landscape full of secrets.

When we arrive at my apartment block, I try to carry my own bags up the six flights of stairs, but the old man waves away my offers of assistance as he ascends. I open the door to my apartment and turn on the light, gesturing for him to step inside. For the first time, I see his full face, his gray hair and tattered jacket collar, and I wonder how long he has lived, how hard he must have worked, and all that he must have experienced as his country fell apart and rebuilt itself over the past decades. I remember that I have not even learned his name, and somehow, for all the intimacy we have shared, this seems wrong. I open my mouth and stammer a hesitant greeting in both Kazakh and Russian.

"Menin atym Jacyntha. Menia zavut Jacyntha."

The old man puts his hand to his heart, bows slightly and answers back, *"Menia zavut Rustem. Ochen pryatno."*

After a few more formalities of payment and thanks, I realize I still have Rustem's blanket wrapped around my shoulders. I take it off and hand it to him, but he simply steps back and shakes his head. With that, he smiles and nods one final time, then turns to go back down the stairs.

My apartment is warm and inviting, and I am awake now and eager to settle in. I flit between rooms, switching on lights and unpacking my bags of silks and spices. From my living room I can see the snow gathering on the roof of the building opposite. In the far distance, a dawn glow is beginning to rise above the mountains. I know that in a few hours Almaty will wake up to a morning full of the new promise that fresh white snow brings and, for the first time since I stepped off my flight from Vancouver in early August, so will I.

Suddenly, I understand: this is a land more ancient, more compelling, than any I have ever known. It is a place driven by the memory of a nomadic world and its rules of hospitality; a world in which complete strangers have to care for each other under the most adverse of circumstances. I understand too that if I am going to live, to really be alive in this ever-changing country, I need to open my heart and embrace kindness as an act akin to breathing, just in the way Rustem showed me tonight.

Only then will I have earned my right to be here.

I doubt I will ever see Rustem again in this city of two million souls, but I fold his blanket carefully and put it in my closet, ready to offer it to a neighbor, friend or stranger who might need comfort and warmth one day. As I do this, an unfamiliar word forms at the base of my throat and slowly escapes my lips. In one soft breath, as dawn nears in a city that has learned to share itself with the mountains and the steppe, I whisper, "*Rahmet*" – thank you.

It is a word I will say every day for the next four years, and I will mean it every time.

Rahmet, Kazakhstan. *Rahmet*.

The Changing of the Seasons

by Erika Rosati

When our family received word of a relocation to Kazakhstan, I, like many others I have since met, had to consult an atlas to determine the whereabouts of our destination. Only then did I realize how vast the Kazakh territory is. Bewildered, I discovered that Kazakhstan is one of the largest countries in the world, and that Astana is one of the youngest – and the coldest – capital cities in the world. From Europe to Kazakhstan... I was to be catapulted into a strange and different world.

I landed in Atyrau in the middle of the summer with my husband, who was immediately dispatched to work in the steppes, and our two daughters, who adapted to this brand-new reality in less than a minute. July in Kazakhstan is a time for holidays, a time of scorching heat, steaming asphalt and semi-deserted cities, and I did my best to get to know my new surroundings while the crowds were away.

In those early days, I walked with the girls along the banks of the Ural River, which here divides Europe and Asia and mixes the different cultures, intrigued by the fishermen who attempted to catch big fish with their rudimentary fishing rods (just a wooden stick with a piece of fishing wire tied to the end) and equipment. On our walks, I stumbled across a new world and a small slice of land that I would never have known had I decided to stay locked indoors. I found a special city that conjures up a whirlwind of emotions.

My grandmother might have felt comfortable here: it feels like a country in a post-war period; it is a vibrant country that is beginning to bloom, as our beautiful Italy did in the 1950s. It is a country that is starting to experience well-being, remember culture, and accept diversity. It is opening to the world now that the communist regime is over, growing and blending with the Western world. Whether this is positive or negative is worth debating, but what is certain, is, that the Kazakhs are a people trying to preserve their traditions in the face of an invasion of consumerism and the media.

The girls and I walked into the depths of the city too, and here we found a playground. Our sanctuary for several days, it was just a swing, a slide and a muddy sandbox where children cooked meals and baked cakes of mud. It was under shade, which is not to be scoffed at in this region in mid-summer; a colourful spot in an unknown city, hidden by the buildings that surrounded it. These were exciting times for us. I was reminded that children are children, no matter where they are, and do not perceive aesthetic differences, while mothers exchange the same knowing looks in every part of the world.

During one of our playtimes we were introduced to a life far removed from our own urban ways. A small van approached and stopped next to the playground. All around us we could feel a growing excitement. Two men got off the truck and unloaded a sheep. The animal was moved to a small space next to the swings and, within an hour, was hung by its feet, killed and skinned. I felt like an intruder and was overwhelmed by a thousand conflicting feelings. I walked away as life in the playground carried on as usual: a barbecue, the back and forth of an iron swing, the cuddling and amusing of a toddler, the stirring of mud soups inside imaginary pots. I later discovered that the sheep was a sacrifice for Hilal, the beginning of Ramadan.

A few days after this experience, the weather began to change, reminding us that our playground days were not eternal. I knew it, as we all did, that it had to happen sooner or later, though I would have preferred the latter. First the scorching heat gave way to a cool breeze, then the sun gave way to the clouds, the rain and the mud. Finally, the real, bitter cold arrived, slowly but radically changing the country to a place without greenery... no flowers, no trees, only a monotonous white landscape and a giant frozen river. The fishermen who had sat on the river banks in the summer now sat on the ice, pierced with their unlikely fishing rods, and patiently waited for the fish to bite. The only feature constant in this city is the clear, beautiful blue sky, which always puts you in a good mood.

My family and I faced the upcoming winter armed with information but were nonetheless unprepared for the reality. We had never been exposed to such low temperatures, and each day a small drama unfolded in our household... thermal T-shirt and pants, shirt, fleece, leggings, pants, jacket, hat, scarf, gloves and boots... putting layer upon layer of clothes on small two girls was a considerable task, one that every mother here had come to learn.

This is how it typically worked: while I dressed my youngest, I urged my other daughter to dress herself. As I was about to finish putting the first layer on my youngest, I would start shouting at the eldest, who had managed to comb and tie her hair, but was still in her pajamas. I'd postpone the dressing of the youngest to help her sister, who would have started crying desperately because, in putting on her shirt, she had messed up her hair. I would resume the dressing of the youngest, meanwhile begging the eldest to stop crying.

"Please get a move on and get dressed," I'd cajole. Jacket, boots, hat, scarf, gloves, backpack... she was finally ready. I would then run to the youngest and help her put on her jacket, boots, hat, scarf, gloves, backpack... Ready!

Shortly after, I would turn and find my youngest stripping.

"I'm too hot," she would say.

I would open the door and take my eldest outside, she grumbling like a pressure cooker because she would have to continue combing her hair on the school bus. I would dress her sister again. Finally, it was my turn: jacket, boots, hat, scarf and gloves. The day could start at last and we headed out.

After a few minutes every part of the body exposed to air would begin a slow freezing process. Then the wind chill would hit the face, the eyes. As shivers ran through our bodies, we pulled at our scarves, even putting on sunglasses for extra protection. The children, however, faced most of this discomfort as if it were nothing new, and a cup of tea or hot chocolate was enough to recharge their batteries.

I will miss all this. There is a poetry and humour to it. I know that the moment I put my feet on Italian soil again, I will feel a bit empty. I will miss Kazakhstan's people, its colors, the blue sky, even the feeling of sadness that grips you when you arrive in a country that is not your own and where you do not feel at home. I will miss the smell of the evenings, the night sky and yes, even the bitter cold.

Translated by: Carlotta Faso

When All Else Fails, Cluck!

by Johanna Means

While strolling near the Ishim River and enjoying the warm, summer weather of Astana, my friends and I decided to try a local restaurant for lunch. Three adults, with three children among us, we had just arrived in Kazakhstan. Although we had read and heard about horse meat and *plov* (a Russian dish with meat, rice and carrots), as well as other traditional entrées, we were at a loss as to what kinds of dishes might be served. Prior to coming to Kazakhstan, we had brushed up on the basics of "hello", "thank you", and "goodbye", along with "good" and "bad". And, of course, we were familiar with *peevah* (beer). None of us understood enough Russian or Kazakh to read a menu, but the restaurant would have a menu in English – right?

We decided on an adorable, outdoor restaurant we had chanced upon. Plants and flowers draped the brick walls, while vines danced across beams over our heads, and the tables and chairs were plastic. It had an amazingly tropical feel, with a small creek flowing by, where swans floated lazily. Latin-influenced music was playing, and for a moment we were unsure if this was an authentic local restaurant. A waitress came over and, much to our surprise, she did not speak English; they did not have a menu in English either. (Of course, we would soon learn that few locals speak English, and those that do have a limited vocabulary, unless they are in a college or academic work setting.)

Let me say here: in Kazakhstan, if you are ever in a hurry, do not *go out* to eat. Kazakhs are laidback at mealtimes and the focus is on enjoying their time together. There is no hurry to eat and be somewhere else. It may be five minutes before your drink order is taken, or it may be 20 minutes. Becoming edgy will not make the service quicker, so learn to relax, and enjoy quality conversation with your companions. Also, do not expect the orders to arrive at the same time. When a dish is ready, it is brought out to you. There is no option of putting it under the heat lamp.

That day, while trying to figure out the menu, the only thing we could recognize was *shashlyk*, a form of shish kebab. We ordered lamb, our preferred choice, but also the only Russian 'animal' word we could remember. It would be easiest to just order what we knew, we thought.

"*Nyet*," our waitress replied. They did not have lamb. It turns out that restaurants will often be out of something on the menu. In fact they will often have one choice available, despite the menu offering four or five options – as was the case on this day. The problem was that we had no idea what this single option was and our waitress was unable to tell us. (We would learn very quickly to have ready a second and third back-up order when eating out.)

My friend Chad, a fellow American, and I stared at each other blankly. We did not have our pocket dictionaries with us. We shared no common language with our waitress. Or did we? Chad looked at her, a young girl of about 19 years, and without giving it much thought, he mooed. She turned red, and we all laughed. She shyly covered her face, and then managed to shake her head, laughing along with us. Not one to give up, Chad made a second attempt.

"Baaahhh," he bellowed.

This time, our waitress laughed out loud, her blush deepening.

"*Nyet*," she repeated.

I decided that I would give it a try.

"Bawk, bawk," I said in my best chicken impersonation.

Our table was in stitches and our waitress, who seemed to be enjoying the game of charades, became excited.

"*Dah!*" she yelled. We had succeeded! We were ordering chicken for lunch.

The main dish out of the way, it was time to tackle the ordering of the side dishes and salads. But we didn't know our colors – and how does one imitate tomatoes or lettuce? Chad had another good idea.

"*Horosho?*" he asked, pointing to an item on the menu. She understood that we wanted her opinion on which salads to try. With an understanding smile, she pointed to several different salad options that she recommended. We decided to try one of each. Why not, right? It was our first eating-out adventure in this new country. About 20 minutes after her arrival at our table, our order had been placed. We weren't entirely sure what we would be eating, but we were confident in our waitress and her suggestions. After all, we had bonded over barnyard noises.

While we waited, the adults enjoyed big, cold drafts of beer. I have since become quite fond of Kruzhka Svezhego Barhatnoe, the local beer, and prefer that to the Belgian or German brews my friends drink when we go out. The kids had ordered juice. In America, when you order this, you get a glass of juice that usually costs more than it is worth, and there are no refills. Here the waitress brought out the entire juice container, much to our delight!

There were a few other patrons in the restaurant, and we had begun to feel as if we were on display. Maybe it was because we looked so different, or because we were speaking

English. Or, perhaps, it was because we were loud and silly (and making farm animals noises). Fortunately, when we made eye contact, pleasant smiles were exchanged. Our lunch was the first of many opportunities to learn how friendly the Kazakh people are.

Our meal finally arrived, and we couldn't have been more pleased. The *shashlyk* was cooked to perfection. Pulling meat off such large metal skewers was a novelty for me (and by large, I mean at least 20 inches long!). One salad consisted of corn, mayonnaise and tomato, another of tomato and cucumber in a balsamic style dressing. A third dish was a variety of roasted vegetables. Prior to arriving in Kazakhstan, I had been worried I would not like any of the food. I had secretly hoped I would lose weight while here, but at that moment, I knew it wasn't going to happen. I had already discovered several things I liked, including the beer.

Our table became suddenly quiet as we savored each new dish. We passed the plates around either until we could eat no more or until the food had completely disappeared. It was a glorious first outing in our new country. Our waitress left us to enjoy the occasion, appearing only when our beers were running low; just the kind of attention we appreciated.

On the way back to our apartments later that day, we continued to have a good laugh over our barnyard antics. I did not let that experience go to waste either. A few weeks later, I was in the grocery store picking out cat food for my very picky and fat furry friend, who had come to Kazakhstan with me. A young man in the aisle saw my confusion and offered to help. He did not speak any English, so I resorted to my best chicken impression. He laughed hysterically, said something about

Americans, and proceeded to show me the chicken flavor. As he walked away, still giggling at my silliness, I realized that I didn't have to speak someone's language to make them smile.

Chapter 2

Kazakh History and Traditions

Mourning on the Steppe:
Kazakhstan's Soviet-era Labor Camps

by Stanley Currier

I felt both excitement and trepidation as the car cut through the vast Kazakh Steppe, speeding through the desert-like land that went on for as far as the eye could see. The occasional buildings that interrupted the otherwise flat landscape either spewed filth into the clear wintry sky or stood long abandoned, relics of the Soviet past. It was December 2011, and I was on my way to the village of Dolinka, 30 miles from Karaganda, Kazakhstan, and over six thousand miles from my hometown of San Francisco, California. I had already lived in Kazakhstan for more than 10 years, but like many of my Kazakh friends, had never been to this area. Thousands of miles away from the oil-rich towns on the Caspian Sea that have put Kazakhstan on the map in recent years, this is a part of the country – and its history – that is rarely visited. I was driving straight to the administrative center of a vast network of labor camps that saw an estimated one million 'visitors' from the period of 1932 to 1959, during the height of Stalin's totalitarian reign of the Soviet Union.

"This is a really depressed place," muttered my taxi driver, Margilan, to me in Russian as we pulled into the village. "There are lots of drug addicts here. That's a women's prison over there to the right," he continued, indicating a crumbling three-storey building that seemed to tower over the small detached homes dotting the land. Some of the houses had fresh coats of paint and satellite dishes whereas others looked as if they'd lost out permanently to history. As we drove through the center of Dolinka, we found the administrative center turned museum of KarLag, or the Karaganda Corrective Labor Camp. The three-storey building looked deceptively modern. It could easily blend into any city as a typical government structure, though the bright red star above the entrance evoked clues to its communist past.

Margilan parked his car and we walked up to the museum entrance. After paying an 800-tenge entrance fee, a young Kazakh woman appeared at our side, looking too official for her age on a Saturday morning in her black slacks and crisp white shirt.

"We don't need a guide," I said. "We'll be fine looking around ourselves."

"Come this way, I'm your escort through the museum," she replied briskly. "And remember, no photography allowed." So much for my idea of pictures or a chance to tour the exhibit freely.

Our tour of the museum started on the first floor with an exhibit of a life-sized yurt depicting peaceful statues of a Kazakh family, the vast steppe pictured on the wall in the background. Nomadic Kazakhs would set up their yurts for months at a time, then fold and transport these to their next seasonal location. This display was presumably to illustrate life before the area was taken over by the Soviets in the 1920s, when nomads were forced to live on collective farms; when a whole way of life that had existed for thousands of years was effectively destroyed in a generation. Further on, the museum's introduction room provided documents and photos outlining the camps' establishment in the 1930s, noting efforts to promote agriculture and industry throughout the region. Though the central administrative functions of the camps were controlled at Dolinka, the actual area of the camps stretched for hundreds of kilometers over the steppe into some of the most remote and bitterly cold swaths of land on earth.

We followed our guide down a flight of steps to the basement. On the way down I noticed carved depictions of prisoners à la Edvard Munch's 'The Scream' along the walls. Somber music began playing on cue.

"This is an isolation cell," said our guide. Peering in, I was slightly taken aback at the depiction of a life-sized prisoner wearing green clothing, standing alone in a dank and windowless room. "And next we're going to see the underground cell."

Crossing the small corridor, I peered into a larger room to see another eerily life-sized mannequin staring up at me from a hole in the ground covered by latticed metal bars.

"Oh my God," I muttered. We then walked into the men's and women's cell rooms, both displaying straw-matted bunk beds, minimal furniture and thin, shabbily dressed mannequins. Though the 'prisoners' looked old, who knows how many years of their lives were taken away by the camps.

"And finally, here's the torture room," our guide stated in a matter-of-fact way, as if she'd just told us about the temperature outside.

I walked inside the room and noticed handcuffs hanging from ceilings and red paint representing blood on the walls. I fought the urge to vomit, and didn't have the heart to ask how many people had passed through this room, and what crime – if any – the punishments were for.

We climbed back upstairs, the haunting music following us. Our first stop was the camp library – a dusty collection of books authored by Stalin's predecessor and the 'founding father' of the Soviet Union, Vladimir Lenin. Margilan picked one up.

"May I?" he asked, to the guide's strict reprimand. I asked if the residents had access to these books.

"They could order two books a month, but most of them didn't have time to read," she stated in her flat-toned voice.

"Why not," I asked.

"They were too busy working," she said.

"Doing what?" I continued.

"Everything," she replied, still without a flicker of emotion in her voice or eyes. "Some people were building or working at the factories, others were tending to animals, and others were involved in agriculture."

Posters on the walls of the library and reception room proudly boasted slogans such as "Join Lenin's Plan for Socialism" or "Uncle Stalin is watching all of his daughters and sons from Moscow". Maps depicting the progress of communism throughout the world provided a fascinating glimpse into a history that still influences countless peoples' mentalities and actions today; even 20 years after the break-up of the Soviet Union.

I was particularly interested in the rooms dedicated to political deportees and statistics regarding different ethnic groups. KarLag and Kazakhstan were literally dumping grounds for ethnic groups from all over the Soviet Union and beyond. From 1936 to the early 1940s, nearly half a million ethnic Germans and over 100,000 ethnic Koreans, who had been living in the far east of Russia, were transported in cattle cars and left on the steppe. Those who survived the journey were joined by Chechen, Ingush, Baltic, Ukrainians, Poles... and the list goes on. I was surprised to learn that nearly 90,000 Lithuanians were exiled to Kazakhstan during this period. I knew that many Lithuanians had been sent as political prisoners to Russian parts of Siberia (my own great-grandfather among the ranks for whom the arduous work and living conditions proved fatal), but didn't know that so many were in Kazakhstan. I scanned the walls of deportees' names for Lithuanians – particularly trying to find the last names of my mom's relatives with whom the family had lost contact during the Cold War. I looked at the life-sized cattle cars on display and tried imagining how people could have made the journey in the bitter cold of winter with little more than the clothing on their backs.

Margilan and I continued our museum tour with two more rooms. The first was dedicated to the Kazakh intelligentsia who had suffered during the Soviet period – and there were plenty.

"Look at that photo," said Margilan, clicking his tongue in sadness.

I gazed up the wall to see a photograph of a young Kazakh professor wearing bifocals and a suit.

What could this man have possibly done, I thought, *that changed his fate from professor to camp laborer and prisoner?* Where was the justice for the thousands of people like him shipped to labor camps – or killed – just for being educated? I wondered if this exhibit so critical to Kazakh history would ever go on tour to the capital city of Astana or cultural and business capital of Almaty, or if it would always intentionally remain isolated here on the Kazakh Steppe.

The last room of the KarLag museum was a decidedly bright and pointed effort to look ahead – a space dedicated to the 20 years of Kazakhstan's independence. Here, one could see books lauding President Nazarbayev's social, political and economic achievements; photos of the president depicting a modern, tolerant and confident Republic of Kazakhstan. Even our guide looked a little more relaxed – whether it was because she was nearly done with one more group of tourists, or whether she'd received some good news from whomever she'd been texting furiously throughout our visit, I couldn't say.

I wasn't entirely satisfied with this room. I wanted to learn more about how KarLag closed and what happened to the prisoners and their descendants – as well as the fate of those who had worked at the camps. Later on, Margilan told me that many of the surviving children and grandchildren still live in the surrounding area. I wondered if the museum employees were among their ranks – and how they had come to terms with their family pasts.

Exiting the museum, Margilan started the car. We were determined to find the nearby cemetery dedicated to the victims of KarLag. We had been told by the museum guards that it was a straight-shot five kilometers down the main village road. Margilan stopped at one point to double-check.

"Do you know where the KarLag cemetery is?" he asked a girl, who was bundled in fur, walking down the street.

"The what?" she asked with an incredulous tone. My search for history on this cold December day clearly wasn't at the forefront of local people's minds. We decided to keep driving. A few kilometers outside the village and driving further into the expanse of the steppe, we came across a small road that was all but buried by snow and saw what looked like the gates of a very small cemetery in the distance.

This can't be it, I thought in disbelief. Walking to the cemetery gates, we noted a wooden sign that said, "Cemetery dedicated to the children and prisoners of KarLag, 1930–1940." A number of simple iron crosses jutted halfway out of the ground into our line of vision, and I wasn't sure what lay under the foot or so of snow in terms of tombstones or monuments.

I snapped several photos at the cemetery, the rusting crosses providing a striking contrast to the blue sky and glittering snow on the ground. Margilan and I didn't talk – the somber effects of the morning magnified the chill of my already cold body. We were both lost in our own thoughts. I reflected on what could possibly drive people to organized acts of mass cruelty such as this. I tried connecting memories of conversations with my grandparents about their relatives' experiences in Siberia with the physical landscape surrounding me. I was sad to realize so many details of my own family history are lost to the Siberian plains, and shuddered as I stood in a space dedicated to children for whom arduous camp conditions proved fatal.

At the center of the cemetery several large gravestones stood in close proximity. One bore a Russian Orthodox cross, but they were all covered in snow that hid the engravings.

"Stanley, I'm going to go warm up the car," Margilan said. "Come whenever you are ready."

I started to follow him, then stopped. Running back to the gravestones, I dusted the snow off one of them. Scanning the words, I read in Kazakh and Russian: "In memory of the innocent victims. This should not be repeated." Blinking back tears, I followed Margilan's footsteps through the snow and joined him for a silent drive back to Karaganda.

Reflections atop Almaty's Blue Ceiling

by Kristina M. Gray

It was a June morning in 2008, and I spent it with my Minnesota friend, Kim, on the top of Kok Tobe, overlooking the city of Almaty. The day promised to turn hot and humid, so we knew to start out early.

This particular time on Kok Tobe, or 'Blue Ceiling' (in some translations, 'Blue Hill') was significant for two reasons. First, I had climbed this foothill in front of the Tian Shan mountain range in the summer of 1993, when the serpentine route up was merely an unpaved, dusty switchback. I had been based here as a Peace Corps trainer – the first year we established Peace Corps in Kazakhstan – and our training site had been housed at the former Communist Party school, further down the hill and to the west of these rolling, green hills. I had regularly gazed into the distance from my fifth-floor balcony to the Blue Ceiling on the horizon, where a broken down, post-Soviet cable car had dangled uselessly. It was also in Kazakhstan that I had met Ken, my future husband. I'd had a love-hate relationship with this formerly communist capital (known then as Alma-Ata) and after I had finished training the 30 Peace Corps volunteers, I hadn't thought I would ever return.

This day was also special because I was reunited with Kim. The two of us had come a long way since graduating on the same day in June of 1990, from the Minneapolis campus of the University of Minnesota. Back then we had shared similar interests, talking long hours on the phone, the usual girl talk. We had lost contact though, our lives taking diverging paths. I had lived in the Washington, D.C. area for three years and then in Kiev, Ukraine for seven years, with summer vacations spent in my hometown.

After being separated by countries and continents for almost 15 years, Kim and I were together again, just like old times. She and her husband had started a family – Kim's life was consumed with raising four children ranging in ages four to 14 – and had lived in a remote village north-west of Almaty in the first half of their stay. Both had learned to speak and write in the Kazakh language. In fact, they had published a book in the language on Kazakh children's tales with morals. Erik was simultaneously pursuing his Ph.D. in anthropological studies with an emphasis on Kazakh cultural proverbs.

I was busy teaching my own Kazakh 'charges' at the KIMEP University, who had taken over the buildings of the former Communist school. The irony of coming full circle, to the same institution where I had trained Peace Corps volunteers 14 years earlier, did not escape me.

The refurbished cable car starts moving its passengers up and down Kok Tobe from 11 am, except on a Tuesday, when it opens at 4 pm – which happened to be the day Kim and I had chosen to go up. We had the Blue Ceiling practically to ourselves.

We turned down a taxi that would have taken us to the top for a hefty fee. As we walked up from the parking lot, we took photos along the way. I captured the vibrant 3-D billboard that warned us to keep the environment clean. We were surrounded by lush green vegetation and peeked at intervals through branches to see Almaty's skyline continue to shrink below us. Coming from the flat-as-a-pancake plains of Minnesota farm country, Kok Tobe seemed like a small mountain to me.

Elementary school children painted with tempera paint on the restraining wall towards the top. They showed off their talents in different themes: horses, flowers, anything that they felt like, and all in bright, festive colors. Totally absorbed in their work, they ignored the American foreigners' chatter becoming louder in the thinning air.

It took a leisurely 45 minutes to climb the foothill, though admittedly I was breathing heavily as we completed our final ascent. Kim and I then sat for hours looking over the valley of Almaty below us, while eating our picnic lunch... an idyllic setting for us to share stories about the Kazakhstan we know and love.

Kazakh superstitions

Kazakh author Mukhamet Shayakhmetov writes in his memoir *The Silent Steppe* that the Kazakhs are a superstitious people. Kim, who has also read the book, could vouch for this and shared some of the superstitions she had encountered while living for over a decade in a small Kazakh village. This experience had given her first-hand knowledge of Kazakh living – very different from the big city life of Almaty, with its glossy veneer. In contrast to this Russified and modernized city, an authentic village (*aul*) consists of a mass of yurts. The Kazakh people traditionally were sheepherders, their livestock grazing the lands hundreds of years ago.

"To keep their homes clear of evil spirits, the Kazakhs will collect a kind of holy grass from the mountains, then burn it and shake the smoke around the house," Kim explained. "It is also considered essential to ensure the home is immaculately clean before going to bed because a messy place will only invite unwelcome evil spirits to come lodge during the night." She added that placing a knife under the *besik* or baby cradle was also thought to ward off evil spirits.

Kazakh versus American notions of mobility

As a mother of four, Kim's orientation naturally involves the home. She observed that, for Kazakhs, life events such as birth, circumcision, weddings and death were very important. Even though the Kazakhs come from a nomadic tradition, their homes or yurts were the center of their universe. That is why I suppose 'leaving on a jet plane' for lands faraway holds less significance for many Kazakhs, whereas for Americans like Kim and me, who come from a land of immigrants, a major life event is to depart for lands unknown to us.

I recall when teaching as a Fulbright scholar at a westernized university in Bishkek, Kyrgyzstan in 1993–1995, that my Kyrgyz dean could not understand the concept of jetlag and it messing up one's sleep cycle. She would appear to be very put out.

"Why can't you Americans disembark from the plane and just jump right in to teach English the day after you arrive?" she would ask. "What's wrong with you? Are you sick?"

My illustrious dean painfully understood jetlag once she had visited the U.S., but this was only after several years of observing Americans sluggishly dragging their feet around her university in their first week of teaching.

Kim also explained that the Kazakh practice of Islam does not take place in a mosque, but rather in the home. Shayakhmetov writes in his book of his mother's eloquent mourning improvisation after the loss of a dear family member. Kim had witnessed first-hand how women memorialize a recently deceased loved one with their amazing musical abilities by inventing a song of grief. She had found the Kazakh women's strains of music in their extemporized expressions of sadness hauntingly beautiful.

Children, memorization and Kazakh proverbs

Americans have their own well-worn saying of, "Children should be seen and not heard," which perhaps harks back to our agrarian society of big families and in which children were disciplined to sit quietly while eating their meals. It was considered only fitting and proper that the adults do all the talking at the table. Kazakhs share this sentiment and young children are encouraged to sit and listen to the older (and wiser) members of the family. In their formative years, Kazakh children are expected not just to listen and learn but also to commit stories to memory. It is also the duty of adults, aged 40 years or older, to use proverbs that they once memorized to explain life lessons to the children.

My experience teaching for a year and a half at a Bishkek university showed me that the Kyrgyz students, who share a similar tradition of oral story-telling, picked up the English language quickly –despite the lack of Western-style textbooks. The young people were simply very good at memorizing and listening to intonation patterns of native English speakers. This is essentially what language learning is all about: listening, memorizing and imitating. I observed that oral skills prevailed over written skills, which require more reading.

Something else Kim had observed was that her Kazakh housekeepers had no concept of how to put books away on a bookshelf. As all knowledge was committed to memory and traditional Kazakhs lived in yurts, moving from place to place according to the seasons, Kazakhs owned few, if any, books.

"My Kazakh helpers would unknowingly put our books back on the shelves upside down," explained Kim, "or with the spine to the inside and not facing out so you could read the title." I suppose those of us who have grown up with access to libraries or books at home, don't realize that people without books would not really concern themselves with how to 'properly' place a book on its shelf.

Forbidden subjects among Kazakhs

Apparently money is not spoken of, nor is a lack of it, although to talk about borrowing money is acceptable. Indeed, nothing regarding the home and personal affairs, such as a parent having trouble with a child or a wife who is beaten by her husband, is allowed to be discussed openly. These topics are forbidden outside the family, and even within the family such topics are hushed up.

Kim told me of a young bride who was being initiated into her new family and had to serve her in-laws.

"If the father-in-law was not happy with the way she served him tea, he could beat her," Kim said, before adding, "It is said the Kazakh bride wears braids, because once married she has no time even to fix her hair." So busy is she with learning all the traditions of her new home under the tutelage of her mother-in-law.

Neighbors and mutual indebtedness

Kim also related the important role neighbors play in Kazakhstan. When Kim's youngest daughter was born and wasn't gaining much weight, her Kazakh neighbor took it upon herself to bring goat's milk around daily to help the baby plump up. Kim wanted to pay her neighbor, but the woman would not hear of it. All she wanted from Kim was a promise of 'insurance': if anything happened to her goat in the future, Kim would pay for the vet's bills.

This reminded me of when I lived in China, where locals try to build *guanxi*, a mutual indebtedness, whereby a person can exact a favor from you on their own terms if they once did something for you. Money does not feature in this system, which is much more intricate and detailed than an 'I'll scratch your back, if you scratch mine' approach.

Some afterthoughts on Kazakh culture

Of course, Kim and I talked about many other things as we sat in the shade of the green mountain, feeling its fresh, gentle breezes. She explained the importance for a man (and woman) to find *kurdas,* others who are born in the same year as him (or her).

"It is as if Kazakh men who share the same birth year are blood brothers," she said. This may have something to do with the ancient cycles of life that the Kazakhs regard as sacred.

We also discussed the apparent need of the Kazakh people to blame another for their misfortunes. I had also observed this tendency of projecting blame onto others in my university setting by some of the Kazakh teachers I worked with. I wondered if it might be a residual mindset of a Soviet tendency to not take responsibility for one's actions.

An example Kim gave was of a Kazakh family with seven girls and three boys, who attributed the death of one of their boys to a Russian, who had just moved into the neighborhood, and had supposedly given the boy the 'evil eye'. Someone else, outside the clan, is held responsible for any sadness visited upon the family.

Reflections on the descent from Kok Tobe

The hours had quickly eluded us, just as they used to in our long-ago phone conversations, and Kim and I knew our precious time together was coming to an end. A mother of four and a university teacher, we had our respective responsibilities to get back to.

By this stage Kazakhs were scattered around the top of our Blue Ceiling. Our picnic lunch was finished and we had gone to a few of the gift shops to buy touristy T-shirts for ourselves or as gifts for family members. We quickly made our descent by retracing our steps on the asphalt pavement, winding down to Kim's car. What a change from when I had first walked this road with other Peace Corps trainers. Many of the shacks and houses had been replaced by posh homes along some of the lower switchbacks.

I cherished our shared experiences of the Kazakh culture we knew and loved. Even so, we both admitted that Almaty was a hard place to live in and the people sometimes difficult to love. That is what made our bond as friends all the more special, as if we two Minnesotans had each other's backs in a land foreign to us.

Nauryz in Kyzylorda

by Roberto Boltri

Early in the morning I am awoken by an uproar coming from the street below: cars and trucks honking and people yelling. I open my bedroom window overlooking the city's Dostyk Square, before stepping out onto the balcony. The square has been transformed into a village of yurts in preparation for Nauryz, a traditional celebration connected with the earth's cycles. The origins of Nauryz go back more than 2,000 years to the pre-Christian and pre-Islamic adoration of Zoroaster.

Curious, I immediately make my way down to the street. I walk among the yurts, the traditional houses of the nomadic Kazakh people. Circular in shape, the structures are supported by flexible wooden sticks and covered by waterproof felt. It is a home that these nomads have known since the beginning of life (Herodotus, the 'father of history', speaks about the yurt in his *Histories*). The yurt's most striking characteristic is its lightness – despite its size, it weighs only 100–200 kilograms – which makes it easy to transport, assisting the nomad's mobility on the steppe. The yurt can also be assembled in a short time (two or three hours). The felt covering protects its inhabitants from both hot and cold weather, from rain and snow, making the home comfortable in every season. On the top of the yurt is a circular hole, which permits the escape of smoke from the fire underneath, in the middle of the floor space. This form of ventilation also allows the nomads to see the sky – thus the gap is called the 'window on the sky'.

But if the yurt is the means for moving and migrating, it is also the place in which the nomads meet and socialize. It is a microcosm of family and community life; a place in which the rules of social life, clans, tribes, roles, sexes and generational hierarchies are played out. This is where the everyday rituals of existence meet mystical behaviors, both shamanic practices and religious ones. Men, women, guests, children… everyone has his or her place. One can only imagine the complex world of affection and emotion that exists here, of the traditions that have been built over the millennia. The yurt is the product of the nomad's culture, but it also reinforces traditions and transfers values from one generation to the next. For centuries, during the cold nights on the steppe, the Kazakh nomads have gathered in yurts, listening to their bards while poems, all orally transmitted, are recited; poems such as the epic *Manas kirghiso* and *Kurgulo kazako*.

In the square, every village has arranged its own yurt, inside which the village representatives are seated in a circle, drinking *chai*. I notice their poverty in their worn-out clothes and in the modest shoes aligned outside the entrance. On the square, women prepare the *samovar* (an ancient water boiler) and cook. Dotted about the area are containers of *kymiz* and *shubat* (horse and camel's milk), appreciated throughout the Asian continent – especially *kymiz*: obtained through the fermentation of mare's milk, it becomes sparkling and slightly alcoholic. This 'sparkling milk' is thought by the nomads to have therapeutic and aphrodisiac qualities. It is also lower in fat than *shubat*. I'm now a regular consumer of both.

In the center of each yurt, on colored carpets, are big plates of *beshbarmak* (a traditional Kazakh dish of horse, beef, camel and lamb's meat, served with dough and sprinkled with onions) and over these tower the black heads of sheep.

Horses and camels are gathered on the square's edge, and I'm immediately drawn to them. The most beautiful horses, in my opinion, are the white ones from Aralsk; their hair is unusually soft to the touch. Seeing a young camel on the back of a truck, I approach. The animal, perhaps ill at ease with the unfamiliar location, spits, hitting his target – my jacket – with great precision. The result is much hilarity.

At the bottom of the square, the old, worn PAZ buses from the Soviet era stand, their bonnets open to cool the engine. Drivers and mechanics are gathered around, as well as passengers technically inexperienced but lavish with advice. The only certainty is that later, in the evening, the vehicles will start with a push from their passengers.

In the square I find every kind of trade and service imaginable. Women crouched, foretelling the future with sunflower seeds… photographers and their mobile props: garlands of plastic flowers, Mickey Mouse puppets and cardboard reproductions of cars.

I cross the square and head towards the theatre. As soon as I enter I feel I have jumped back 70 years, to the time of Lenin's NEP. In the hall is a photographic exhibition of socialist labor heroes, typically Asiatic portraits with chests full of medals, honorary diplomas and enrollment cards of the USSR Communist Party and Komsomol, the Communist Youth League.

The next gallery depicts glorious harvests of wheat, rice and cotton, followed by images of the cotton harvests at the beginning of the disastrous receding of the Aral Sea, the reason for my presence here as an ecologist. In the center of the room is a television screen that broadcasts footage of old party and trade union meetings. Nobody watches, but it must remain as a reminder of a past that nobody here seems to regret.

This celebratory exhibition suggests the old Soviet system was not all bad, especially in the services provided in the cultural and social sectors (schools, hospitals, transportation, theatres, cinemas). The system also managed to maintain peaceful coexistence, and sometimes solidarity, among the 130 minority groups of Kazakhstan. Nowadays, the general trend of both the international community and the ex-USSR populations seems to be a total rejection of the past. Only the elderly appear to see clearly the limits of the past but also the limits of the present. Everyone else reaches out to the future, with its promises of consumption. The fact that capitalism also has deep faults is neglected. For example, average life expectancy dropped by three to five years in countries of the former USSR after the transition from communism to an open market.

In my ideal world, elements of the past would be recovered and adapted to this new transition society, to its democracy. These new economic rules would not be solely based on the market, but also include social dynamics, in a new, revised form of 'the welfare state'.

After 10 years of having lived in different countries, including the former Yugoslavia and Uzbekistan, my greater fear is not the rebirth of communism – which I think improbable – but inexorable, unstoppable consumerism. To extend a Chinese proverb: if communism has been a skin disease, consumerism may quickly become a heart disease. Consumerism, inspired by Western culture, risks making Asia – cultural, sophisticated and wise – rough, violent and too quick to compromise in its rush to accept Western consumer-driven ideals.

The Cultural Heritage of Kazakhstan

by Annemarie van Klooster

I always wanted to go to Asia, with its high humidity, green landscapes and friendly people. And yet Kazakhstan – central Asia – is not the Asia I had imagined. I still remember the endless horizon when I first landed in the country and looked out onto the steppe: there were no trees, no houses and, honestly, no green at all. It felt so empty. I'm from a small town in Holland that is surrounded by meadows, so you can imagine how desolate the landscape looked to me. But there was also something magical about it, because I could see the 'end' of the world, far away in the distance.

We don't have camels in the suburbs of Holland. We have cows and horses safely grazing behind fences. Here, camels roam around freely. They belong to someone, of course, but are free to come and go as they please. They graze on small patches of grass growing in the shade of apartments, or under trees, and often they eat from the garbage bins.

Another difference is that we use the Roman alphabet, while the Kazakhs use the Cyrillic alphabet, which looks to me like gobbledygook! I had made sure our children got English lessons before we left Holland because they would be going to an international school, but I had forgotten about Kazakh lessons for myself. How was I supposed to communicate in this country? A dictionary wasn't enough to get by and the language course I had been expecting from the company was not provided. In the beginning, I felt too intimidated to find a teacher. And because I didn't expect to be in Kazakhstan for very long, I thought, *What is the point?*

However, what I regret most is how long it took me to understand the people. If you are going to live in Kazakhstan, or any other part of this world, learning the language is so important. It's the only way to integrate into the local community and start to feel at home. I did try to integrate in my own way, sometimes even by making a fool of myself. If I needed beef or chicken and *not* horse meat from the butcher's, I pretended to be a cow or a chicken. As you can imagine, the staff had a good laugh at my expense.

I was always being asked where I came from and I'd proudly tell them I was from *Golandia* [Holland]. This would make the men smile…

"Aaahhh, Ruud Van Nistelrooy!" they'd say.

Football is not my cup of tea, but fortunately I do know the name of one of our best strikers.

The locals knew other things about Holland too. Amsterdam's red light district and, of course, tulips. I was even told that tulips originally came from Kazakhstan! I also learned that Adam and Eve's garden was allegedly in Kazakhstan. The apple that led to their downfall is supposed to have come from the Almaty region, or so the story goes.

The Kazakh people are very proud of their country. Unfortunately, after the period of Russian communism, the newer generations entered what I call 'the plastic period', with an increased demand for synthetic materials. In the two-plus years I have been here, I have seen several old buildings with beautiful wooden window frames and walls with cane as insulation being destroyed. It pains me that local residents and local government don't realize the value of these houses. It's their history and they can never replace it.

This approach is part of their development though. The country is growing fast, with international companies spending lots of money. People are now able to live a more 'western' life. There is also an internet service, broadening their view and showing them other possibilities. They want to have it all, and I can't blame them! I remember myself at 18 years of age, with the first paycheck I'd ever earned. I wanted everything, which sometimes resulted in a distressingly empty bank account. Here you experience something similar; in many electronic stores you see more counters that grant credit than counters with regular pay terminals. This results in big loans that are never paid off. The interest rate is half that of Holland, but the products are expensive. A car in Kazakhstan costs the equivalent of a car in Holland, and houses are not cheap either.

With loans to pay off every month, people can't spend money on maintaining their houses; in many cases, what is broken will stay broken. The local government and landlords don't spend a lot of money on maintaining properties, or on green areas around the apartments or houses. Luckily, in some areas very old houses do remain, though not always in the best shape. In the past century some great architects must have lived here, and we can only hope the owners realize this before destroying architectural jewels!

Something there's plenty of here though is meat. This spoiled Dutch girl doesn't like to eat anything that looks like the animal it came from, so it was a shock to see the heads of sheep and cows lying under the counter at the butcher. On the upside, when the heads were in stock I didn't have to "moo" anymore to get a piece of beef, as it lay next to the cow's head. I could see the tongue, and I think the heart and some other unknown parts. I knew one thing: I would not bring my children to this store. I was afraid they would never eat meat again.

At the Nauryz celebration, the holiday that celebrates the first day of spring, Muslim Kazakhs kill a cow or sheep and share the meat with the poor people around them. One morning, I was in the gym on the third floor of our building, looking into the garden of the mosque. It was crowded and I saw a lot of animals fastened to the gate. I had no idea why the animals were standing there – until I looked harder and saw a group sitting around an animal, praying and then taking out a knife to slit its throat. Supermarket meat in Holland doesn't look like an animal anymore and it is forbidden to kill an animal without narcosis. That's not necessarily how it should be, but it is what I am used to. Of course, I wanted to save the animal, but it also occurred to me that perhaps the Kazakhs live closer to nature.

When I got home I saw the workers from our compound unloading a sheep. Until my mosque experience that morning I would have thought they were going to start a children's farm in our compound! Later, we were invited by the landlord and the compound staff to celebrate Nauryz with them in the two big yurts that had been set up in front of the compound. I didn't tell my children that the cute sheep they had seen earlier was now their dinner. We danced and ate and enjoyed our first experiences sitting in a yurt and drinking camel's milk… Mostly, we enjoyed being a part of their tradition.

The new generation of Kazakhs might not hold on to their architectural heritage, but they do retain their traditions and share these with others – even with a silly Dutch girl who never learned to speak their language. I may have felt lonely when I came to this country, but I will not feel lonely when I leave. Thank you for giving me this experience Kazakhstan.

Sunset on the Caspian Sea

by Machteld Vrieze

Years after I had gotten married, a young girl from a remote village in Kazakhstan gave me a deeper understanding of what is one of the greatest passages in life... Marriage appears to be a journey in two directions: you move away from home to start a new life, but at the same time you return home, to the comforting traditions and unspoken beliefs of your own family, your place of upbringing, and your culture. I do not recall having had many thoughts on the true origin of my wish to marry a particular man, in a certain tradition. Love was my reason, but now that I, her expat employer, have been invited to this Kazakh girl's wedding, I have been confronted with my own prejudices and beliefs.

By Kazakh standards, Nurgul, a lively 20-year-old, is ready for marriage. She is fluent in both Kazakh and Russian and she has strong opinions and witty answers. I can tell this from the vivid conversations with the other nannies at the weekly playgroup.

Although it is uncommon amongst Kazakh women to discuss boyfriends, I asked Nurgul occasionally about her fisherman from a Caspian Sea village. I tried to listen openly, but reluctantly admit I had to suppress my cultural beliefs that a woman should wait longer for marriage, to prepare for an independent future and maturity to ensure a better decision. But really, what colors my perspective? That an early marriage is a waste of a smart and lively woman because she comes to live a less public life? Why should a couple in love consider the fact that, statistically, marriages between people in their mid-twenties have a better chance than earlier marriages? For what is a better start of a marriage: a statistically proven improved chance at life-long marriage, or the gut feeling that you are so lucky to have found your partner?

So, I just listened, a smile of recognition on my face, to how she met him at her parents' café and how, despite her vow to leave the village life for a promising future, she could not resist this fellow who "would do things for her". Maybe he drove her to a spot to watch the sunset on the Caspian Sea, or kept the best catch of the day for her. He pleases her. It made me think about what a woman needs from a man. In a different part of the world, the same desires remain in women in their youth: the longing to be loved, to see places, to play an important role. When, or if, it turns out differently, one regrets, accepts, or tries to change one's mind.

Perhaps over-sensitive to cultural differences, I did not dare to ask her about finishing her education and her future role in his family. Was I afraid to be proven right, that the world was going to lose this girl to a submissive role? Perhaps while preparing meals together, I could have mentioned some of my so-called 'modern' ideas on the equality of men and women. Perhaps I could have tried to convince her that she could easily earn a good living in the booming city, and that her fisherman would make a great stay-at-home dad. She would laugh out loud, and silently mock me; I certainly am not living this example.

Unaware of my mind wrestling, Nurgul meanwhile contemplated how to pickle the boiled fish or cook the sheep for her future father-in-law and brother-in-law at the engagement party. Knowing she was going to be part of something big, she daydreamed, thinking of the moment she would be unveiled by her closest companions, who will walk her in before her husband, her parents and hundreds of their guests. She will look stunning in her traditional wedding dress and pointed hat with white fur; her hair extended to braids down to her hips and her skin fair as mid-winter. (Poor Nurgul has been wearing suffocating clothes for four hot months, in order to have the fairest skin possible). Her groom will stare at her solemnly, just as she will not smile on this most beautiful day of her life. What would everybody think if she looked happy to leave her house and move to another family?

At Kazakh weddings, sometimes the Master of Ceremonies will invite the couple for a game that predicts the harmony of the future household. They pair up with their backs to each other and have to answer questions as they take a step forward: questions such as, "who will drive the car, who will cook, who will light the barbecue, who will get up at night for the baby, who will earn money?"

Hesitations, double steps or no steps will be met with amused cheers. If I were to play such a game about roles with my husband, we would walk out of the room on each other. Our roles are constantly changing and renegotiated.

As the big day approaches, Nurgul and her fisherman-friend have plenty on their minds. She will soon receive her dowry jewelry, and then they will have to make more family visits; prepare two weddings; book the restaurant (the only one in the village), the dancers, the Michael Jackson act and the *dombra* player; find two dresses (a Kazakh embroidered dress and a big white one) and make pickles and jams until dawn from donated fruits and vegetables.

My husband and I will attend one of her weddings with at least 200 other guests for a full night of eating, vodka drinking, speeches and entertainment. Attending a wedding is always a good time for some contemplation, but this young girl has confronted me just by telling her story. After all, I have found similar beliefs and universal truths about love and marriage in Kazakhstan and the Netherlands. One thing I particularly respect about the Kazakh culture is this: love and marriage are not taken lightly and they know how to mark the occasion by throwing a once in a lifetime celebration!

Chapter 3

City Living in Kazakhstan

Dromophobia

by Laura McLean

The transition to my new Kazakh lifestyle had been relatively smooth. I was so pleased with myself for adapting so quickly, considering I knew next to nothing about the country before I moved here. I had been expecting my adjustment to a Kazakh lifestyle to be an emotional rollercoaster with culture shock and homesickness. Over time, I realized that there was only one thing that stood between me and a comfortable, happy life in Kazakhstan. It wasn't the language barrier, or the strange new foods, or any of the other anxieties that I'd had prior to moving. It was the streets of Almaty that caused me the greatest stress.

My first memorable car ride was on my first day of teaching, when a driver from the school came to pick me up from my apartment on the edge of the city. I cringed as he weaved in and out of the lanes, honking the horn as often and as absent-mindedly as one might use a turn-signal. I realized quickly that the lines painted to divide the lanes of traffic were merely a suggestion, as many people straddled them until they had decided which path was moving faster. A road with two lanes therefore held more than enough room for three lanes of traffic. Other vehicles changed lanes without so much as a sideways glance, veering towards our car and nearly making contact. I was convinced I was going to die in a fiery blaze before I even got to see the campus of the school I'd be working at. Meanwhile, the driver was happily sharing his English vocabulary with me.

"*Sobaka*, dog," he said, pointing to a dog outside, and I nodded as I tried to unclench my jaw enough to smile.

Future car rides were no less traumatic. Every morning he came to pick me up, and every evening he took me home, and all the while I was clinging to the handle of the door and pumping an invisible brake on the passenger side of the car. I did not want to die. Still, it *was* a comfort to have someone from the school help me to and from work every day. Unfortunately, this luxury was not to last. I had been warned that, once introduced to the bus system, I would either be taking a bus or cabbing it to school. I dreaded the idea of being left to fend for myself on these busy streets. I did not believe I would be able to recognize my stop from a bus, and I certainly was not ready to take a gypsy-cab.

Gypsy-cabs are unauthorized taxis. Anyone with a car can be a gypsy-cab; they simply need to choose a fare and negotiate a price and destination. When I first heard about this, I thought it sounded very close to what I would consider hitch-hiking. Since hitch-hiking is illegal in Canada, I had never flagged down a stranger's vehicle and crawled into their back seat. I did not want my first time to be in Kazakhstan, of all places. However, I was assured repeatedly that this was the way Kazakhs got from Point A to Point B, and I was determined to avoid looking like a prissy Westerner. When the time came for me to hail my first cab, I was beyond nervous. I had been given all the advice I needed to survive my first trip, and now it was time to put this into action. The ladies at the school had given me the 'golden rules to gypsy-cabbing':

"Don't get into a car with two men, that's trouble. Negotiate the price *before* you get into the car, but don't pay him until *after* you get there. Pay in exact change, or you won't get any money back. And whatever you do... don't get in the car with a woman driver."

I have since broken each of these rules at one time or another, and lived to tell the tale. But that first time I followed the Gypsy-Cab Rules to the letter. I hailed my first driver, told him the name of the intersection I lived on, and held up five fingers to tell him I would pay 500 tenge. He nodded, and I climbed into the seatbelt-deprived backseat, waiting for my adventure to begin. He drove off at lightning speed, and I watched out the window, hoping to see a landmark of some kind that would assure me I was not being kidnapped. Not surprisingly, I didn't have a clue where we were headed. He tried to carry out a conversation with me as we drove, and I repeated my only Russian phrase at that point, *"Ia ne ponimayu!"* ["I don't understand!"] He eventually gave up, and only the sound of Russian techno music and honking cars were left to keep us entertained. I got out of the car, pleased with myself for having braved the stranger's vehicle.

As time went on, I realized that gypsy-cabs were not something to be feared, but a really amazing social opportunity. After a while, when I had started taking Russian lessons, I realized that these cabs gave me the chance to practise the language, and to learn a few things about Kazakhstan as well.

On one of my rides downtown, my driver was a charming elderly man who wanted to know everything about Canada. He teased me because I don't play ice hockey; I only like to watch it. He told me that simply wasn't good enough. He asked, sincerely, if I had an American passport. I told him that Canada has its own passport, and he found that fascinating. I knew right away that this was going to be a cultural exchange, in which we both learned something new about the other's country.

From there, the ride also became a bit of a language lesson for both of us. He spoke enough English to say, "My name is…"

and, "I am from Almaty." He asked if English was the official language in Canada, and I informed him that we spoke French as well. He broke out into his only French phrase: "*Merci!*"

"*Merci, merci beaucoup!" he continued before asking, puzzled, "Shto 'beaucoup'?"* ["What is *beaucoup*?"]

I told him the Russian translation, and he was so excited with his new word.

"Laura, I love you *beaucoup!*" he yelled out. He was having a ball, and I spent the majority of the ride in fits of laughter. I didn't understand the conversation entirely, but from what I did understand, he had invited me to his house so his wife could cook *beshbarmak* for me. I told him I was on the way to see friends, and he seemed genuinely disappointed.

The best part of the ride was when he answered his phone, and I heard my name amidst the Kazakh babble. He then passed his phone to me and a voice on the other end said, "'Allo! Laura, 'allo!" I said hello into the phone, and the person on the other end said, "'Allo", and then I sat there in silence, wondering what I was expected to say next. I wasn't sure whom I was even talking to! I burst out laughing, and handed the phone back. This was a great game for him. He grabbed the phone, carried on in Kazakh, and again I heard my name.

On the way out of the door, I shook his hand and told him that it was very nice to meet him. He gave me a peck on the hand, and I laughed to think how this type of cab ride would never happen in Canada. I have never been introduced to the driver's friends over the phone, let alone invited to his house for a home-cooked meal. It was amazing how, after a short 20 minutes in this man's car, I felt like I had made a friend.

I quickly discovered that a fixation of cab drivers in Kazakhstan is marital status. Many conversations have started with the driver asking me where I am from, if I like living in Almaty, and whether or not I am married with children. Initially, I would try and carry out the conversation as honestly as possible, but as I still cannot explain myself completely, it is sometimes easier to lie a little.

One man was determined to discover the underlying reason why I was not married. He asked me if I had a husband, and I gave him what I had been told was the acceptable answer.

"Not yet!" I replied.

He asked me if I had a boyfriend.

"Not yet!" I confessed, again.

He raised his eyebrows at me in the rearview mirror, trying to figure out the reason for my lack of commitment at the ripe old age of 23. He thought of a possibility.

"Lesbian?" he asked me.

I informed him in Russian, as best as I could, that I was not a lesbian, but he remained curious. From what I could determine, he then asked me, "You marry a woman?"

I was unsure if this was a question directed at my culture as a whole, or at me, as an individual. I tried to clarify his question, so he rephrased.

"You have a wife?"

I told him I did not, and he raised his eyebrows at me again in the mirror. It was clear that I was not giving him answers that he liked, so he started back at the beginning of the conversation.

"Where is your boyfriend?" he asked me in Russian. I sighed deeply.

"China," I told him. "My boyfriend is in China."

He smiled and nodded, and I knew that this fake international romance was more acceptable than being willingly and openly single.

Since this ride, I have discovered that a more effective way of redirecting the conversation is to ask about the driver's family instead. Many wallets have been whipped out to show me pictures of families. I have heard stories about the brother who moved overseas, and the daughter who is fluent in English. The pride to be had in having a family is contagious, and I soon find myself discussing my parents and siblings back home as well.

Since my initial months in Kazakhstan, my fear of driving these streets has decreased greatly. The truth is, that something that initially caused me so much grief is now one of my favourite things about living here. I can see the roads for the organized chaos that they truly are, and the absence of fear has allowed me to see each gypsy-cab trip as an opportunity. Nearly every ride I have taken with a total stranger has been an experience. We've learned things about each other's cultures, shared stories and laughter, and exchanged the whole-hearted and honest words, "*Ochen pryatno*… nice to meet you!"

The Magic *Dvor*

by Laura Kennedy

In Almaty, the courtyard (*dvor* in Russian) is the center of social life for the apartment block. Ours is unlike most in the leafy former capital: once used for parking, it is not much more than a stark concrete space. When we debated moving into the building almost three years ago, I viewed the *dvor* as a distinct liability. There is neither grass nor trees. A small playground structure stands off in one corner, dwarfed by the 16-storey towers that surround it. The center is punctuated by a few wooden benches; small flower boxes dot the perimeter in an attempt to lend seasonal color to an otherwise dreary setting.

And yet I soon learned that our courtyard may not be much to look at, but the vibrant life that is lived in the *dvor* and the joy it gives to the children who play there, be they Kazakh, Russian or American, cannot be rivaled.

The new arrivals

I first noticed our *dvor* was special when we brought our girls to see the new apartment. Stepping through the gate, we were almost immediately approached by curious, friendly children. Who were these new girls? Did they speak Russian and most important, were they ready to play? Our previous place, one of the new, so-called 'elite' buildings, with its manicured garden, fountain and draconian security, had been nothing like this.

Once we had moved into our new building, we started to notice the pattern of life in the *dvor*. During the day, the lack of shade can make it unbearably hot, particularly in summer. On school days only a few mothers and grandmothers wander out with baby carriages. But by the time evening rush hour in Almaty nears its peak, our *dvor* comes alive with activity. Toddlers negotiate their first steps while dodging scooters and bouncing balls. In the center, the little girls hold court with their bicycles, deciding who will chase and be chased today. The bigger girls, already leggy and showing universal signs of 'teenage attitude', are playing word games, sketching chalk portraits on the asphalt, talking about friendships. On the benches, nannies keep one eye on their charges while exchanging small talk in Russian and increasingly, in Kazakh. Brothers and fathers read the paper patiently while their little ones beg for just a few more minutes of playtime before going in for dinner.

In the corner of the *dvor* nearest my entryway, a mob of boys of all ages engages in a joyous romp with a football. These are the boys whom I encounter most evenings after work. They invariably hamper my entrance to the building, but I don't mind. Their laughter and positive energy take the edge off a stressful workday.

Playing inconspicuously among these children, who are mostly Kazakh but with a few Russians and other nationalities of the Kazakhstani melting pot, are my two American daughters. They play games that seem much like those of my own childhood in the US, but with a Central Asian twist and Russian names like *klassi* (hopscotch), *pryatki* (hide-and-seek) and *svetafor* (red light, green light; literally 'traffic lights'). In the *dvor* our girls are learning a vocabulary that cannot be taught in a classroom.

Most evenings and weekends, when the weather is good, the apartment intercom rings with a steady stream of kids calling our girls out to play. They jump with excitement at the sound of the bell, each hoping that the call will be for her.

Then begins the ritual of grabbing the bicycles, cries of, "Wait for me!", shoes, a jacket, an object for show-and-tell, or some other novelty to take outside.

Parents returning home from a hard day's work are treated to a celebrity welcome in our *dvor*. Waving from the top of the slide, whizzing by on scooters, bicycles and skateboards, we hear: "*Zdravsvuite*!" ["Hello!"], "*Privet*!" ["Hi!"] and even the occasional, "Hello!" from those who know we are American. Then inevitably, "*Veedut lee Amely i Fya?*" ["Will Amelie and Fia come out?"]

The *dvor* is a magnet for kids from the small, neighboring apartment buildings. The bespectacled Ablai, a kind and gregarious nine-year-old, can regularly be seen squeezing through the gates to our courtyard, usually with his younger mischievous brother in tow. A still younger brother follows, with the nanny bringing up the rear. These kids have no playground of their own, so they cross the driveway to ours. No one seems to mind – the more the merrier.

Though most of the time we are just another family in the building, sometimes there is no escaping our American roots. When spring arrived during our first year in the *dvor*, we decided to take out our baseball mitts for a game of catch. We were soon surrounded by curious kids, all wanting a turn to try on the glove and play. The next trip home we bought some extra gloves to expand the game. Trips back to the States for holidays also mean bringing back to Kazakhstan 'exotic' American favorites like candy canes or root beer barrels. The girls are eager to introduce these to the kids in the *dvor*.

For some reason, Fia recently decided to teach the song '99 bottles of beer on the wall' to her friends. To make it work in Russian, she changed the wording a bit, but we now like her version better than the original:

"99 bottles of beer on the floor,
99 bottles of beer;
You pick one up and throw it at the wall,
98 bottles of beer on the floor!"

Friendships come and go in the *dvor*. Families move, kids outgrow old friends and form new alliances. Diyana, the pint-sized pistol who has been a fixture in the *dvor* as well as in our apartment for the past two and a half years, has left us recently. Her family moved to a new apartment about a mile away. For most kids, such a move would signal the end of the friendship. In Almaty we are lucky, however; *azhe* (grandmother) lives just downstairs, and we know we will always see Diyana on Sundays when she comes to visit.

Not your average mini-market
Many evenings, groups of kids run to the small market adjacent to our apartment block for a small treat: ice cream, a lollipop or the locally popular *sukhariki* (dried bread cubes that come plain or in flavors like cheese and sausage), or packets of *semechki* (roasted sunflower seeds). The mini-market and the produce stand next to it are an extension of our *dvor* and just as full of life and color.

The owners of the mini-market are from southern Kazakhstan, the Shymkent region near the border with Uzbekistan. They know all the regulars from our building. It's the kind of place where, if you are short a few tenge today, you can pay next time; a place where the clerks remember which kind of chocolate your kids like and remind you when you haven't bought a treat for them lately.

My youngest daughter is partial to the fresh potato pies, or *pirozhky*, that the store makes and sells for about 30 US cents each. When we pull into the small driveway that separates the store from our building, the girls clamor for a few tenge to buy something for themselves, then head straight away to the *dvor* to play. Often they buy extras to share with their friends, and their friends do the same. Sharing is a way of life in the *dvor*.

On the street outside the store, past the ice cream freezers that tempt customers with frozen treats year round, Arstan, the produce man, talks to me frequently about language and culture. He says he admires how well the girls speak Russian. He says he and his wife speak Kazakh at home and that sometimes Russian is a challenge for them too.

We talk about which apples taste best – I tell him in America I don't like the red ones that look picture-perfect but taste like sawdust – and he waxes nostalgic that the Aport apples for which Almaty was once famous have disappeared from the city, the orchards having given way to overpriced housing developments. Recently, on a day when an aggressive customer kept me waiting for service, Arstan lamented that in the bustling city, some locals have lost their sense of politeness.

This year I watched as Arstan and his crew painstakingly stuck large letters onto their canopy facing our *dvor* – a colorful sign in Russian read, 'Vegetables – Fruits.' The next day all of the letters had been torn down from the canopy. I had a hunch that this was not an act of vandalism.

"Look over there," I said to my girls, "the letters have been torn down. I bet they got into trouble because the sign was in Russian but not in Kazakh."

A day later the sign reappeared, this time in two languages – Kazakh in large letters on top, with Russian in smaller letters underneath – evidence of the pro-Kazakh language policy in action.

Goodbye for the summer

Last week marked the end of the school year and the day was bittersweet: my daughters and husband were to leave early the next morning for summer vacation. I would not see them for more than a month while they spent time in the US with their grandparents. In the evening the girls asked to play outside with their friends. While I desperately wanted them to spend these final hours before their vacation with me, I decided to let them savor their time in the *dvor*.

Like most other summer nights, my daughters stayed out until the very last child was called home. They came home tired and satisfied that they had played till the end. Then, as they were washing up, the doorbell rang. A girl of 11 or 12 stood outside, asking for Fia. When my daughter came to the door, the girl held out a pen and pencil.

"This is a gift for you, to remember me by," she said.

During our eight-plus years in Almaty, we have always chosen to live in apartments: to afford ourselves a more 'walkable' urban lifestyle and to allow our children to socialize more easily with local kids. When I am having my occasional doubts about our lifestyle choice, about not giving my girls the joys of a house and backyard, I think about these moments and know I have made the right decision. I think about the girl standing at our door with pen and pencil. I remember how my daughter described our *dvor* to relatives in America, not as an overheated and barren concrete slab, but as a fantastic play area "with the most beautiful flowers you have ever seen". I think about the surge of positive energy I get each evening from the football boys. I think about Diyana's smile and about my conversations with Arstan. I think about a place that often seems frozen in time with its simplicity and innocence, our safe haven from the stresses of contemporary life.

These are the images that form the richly textured multicultural landscape of my day-to-day life in Almaty. Even more than the dramatic mountain landscape, the *dvor* is the place we will remember most fondly. This is the place where my children learned to bike and skate, about sharing and compromise, and where they learned about the strength and kindness of the Kazakh people. In the *dvor*, in our magic *dvor*, they are having the time of their lives.

Celebrating Art in Atyrau

by Alejandra Reyes

What have you heard about this huge country located in the heart of Eurasia? My family and I arrived not knowing much at all – just that we were to spend three years here, based in Atyrau, a small city near the Caspian Sea. In that time I had the opportunity to travel all over Kazakhstan, and what impressed me and my kids the most was the country's variety of exceptional natural landscapes: spacious steppes; mountains, such as Khan Tengri or the Zailijsky Alatau range; and lakes, like the Balkhash, the only lake in the world with both fresh water (in the west) and salt water (in the east).

When we first arrived though, I didn't know what to do with myself... I felt disoriented. The kids were enrolled in a lovely little school with other children of all nationalities, but arriving in such a different place, to an alien language with letters and sounds I had never heard before, was a challenge for me. In the beginning, I spent entire days learning simple words and trying to figure out how to request items in the supermarket! Once I had set up all the basic needs – and by basic I mean only food and water – I realized the rest would be taken care of by the company that had brought us to Kazakhstan. But even when I started to participate in coffee meetings with other expat women, something was missing... I missed my old life as a cultural administrator, a career I had found by chance after I had the opportunity to be an assistant at an exhibition in the MNBA, the Chilean National Museum of Fine Arts.

One day I asked my driver to take me to a local art academy, where I asked to speak to an art teacher. A lovely woman who spoke English well, showed me to a door. I knocked.

A secretary behind a little desk asked me to wait and I sat for about 20 minutes in the teacher's peach-colored room. He was a painter with vast experience; a member of the Artist League of Kazakhstan, and a long time teacher at Maaly Art Academy. As he entered the room, I noticed his dark wild hair, which fell to his shoulders. His name was Adilhayer Pangerevic. I didn't realize at the time how important this meeting would turn out to be.

I started my drawing lessons in Adilhayer's studio, a big room divided in two; one part for students and a smaller section for his own works, where he had almost 70 paintings and a few sculptures. One of my favorite sculptures was a piece of wood in the shape of a horse, which he had decorated with some metal pieces and stones.

Twice a week I spent my mornings in front of a huge window that overlooked the Atyrau White House, a government building beside the Ural River, one of the oldest rivers in the world. Every day brought a different view. In winter the panorama was white – has white ever been so amazing? If you sharpened your vision, you could see all the colors of the spectrum in the snow. Water fell from some pipes, freezing on the spot and becoming sharp icicles hanging from the roofs. It was an image stuck in time, as if in a photograph.

I committed those mornings to memory as they gave me the peace of mind and the inspiration I needed to do my drawings. I sketched for hours, looking out at that peaceful scene, listening to the pianoforte being played in the next room by young students learning symphonies by the great composers. The world stopped for a moment and warmth filled my heart.

My technique in drawing human figures and sculptures was slowly developing. My perception and analyses of the objects I drew had improved; so too had my point of view, shadows and textures. Sometimes I had a young student modeling for me for hours! I was surprised, because no one in my country would do this. It can only happen in a place where people are used to living life at a different pace, with other priorities.

Kazakh people are quiet; they don't show much emotion, smile, or make gestures when first meeting, but with time and after gaining their trust, they become more relaxed and enthusiastic – especially during official celebrations such as Nauryz and Victory Day. The Kazakhs are descendants of the Mongol Empire, which incorporated a vast area of Central Asia and extended into what is Western Europe today. Nomadic tribes, they are the survivors of the Siberian Steppes. They are excellent warriors and not easily conquered. They preserve the distant memory of the original founding clans through traditions and oral history – and they are very proud of their culture. Kazakh artists tended to paint mythological characters of Kazakh history and the wildlife of the steppes. In visual arts, heroes, political leaders, musicians and poets are the most represented.

After about six months of almost religious dedication to my drawing lessons, I realized many of Adilhayer's colorful images of tigers, horses, women and unknown faces, surrounding me every day, had given me the inspiration I needed. I realized how talented my teacher was. I realized also that my first impression of him, as a serious and hard-talking person, had been mistaken. After spending time drawing with him, I had come to know him as a kind, sensible, and intelligent man.

One day, I broke the silence in the room.

"Adilhayer, what would you think if I organized an exhibition of your art works?" I asked.

He looked at me, doubtful, so I explained what I had studied and what I had done before, and how I envisioned the exhibition. By the end of our conversation, he had agreed.

I started to meet with people who I thought could collaborate on the project, and I asked around art academies for assistance – without any success. Time went by, summer arrived, and the children finished the school year in Atyrau. My family and I left for the holidays, but I could think only about coming back to "Aty", as I had started calling it.

On my return, Adilhayer and I finally found a sponsor, with the help of another artist, the Scottish photographer Robert Kerr. We were three volunteers of three nationalities sharing one language: a love for communicating the Kazakh culture through the arts. After endless meetings, agreements and phone calls, Agip KCO, an Italian oil company in Kazakhstan, agreed to sponsor our long-awaited art exhibition. They would provide the venue and they would pay for the refreshments and invitations. It was the first time that Agip had sponsored an art event in Kazakhstan, so I felt extremely fortunate.

Adilhayer and I met frequently to talk about oils, techniques, measurements, and to decide on the exhibition details. We had around 70 paintings at our disposal. In order to select the final paintings, I grouped them into size and type: portraits, landscapes, still life pieces and figurative paintings. Finally, we decided on 36 oils, all of them beautiful pieces of art that showed the spirit of the country.

The exhibition was to be hosted at Chagala Club House. *Chagala* is seagull in the Kazakh language and, when springtime arrives and the weather becomes warmer, you often see these sea birds flying over the Ural River. I liked this space in the Club House because it had big windows all along the wall, so the lighting was excellent.

On the day of the opening, the paintings were in place and the TV was ready to play a short film showing all of Adilhayer's artwork. I had arranged for a journalist and a photographer to cover the opening ceremony. The guests started arriving at 7 pm with Adilhayer and me standing at the main door welcoming everyone, really pleased with the turn out.

I had the chance to meet two of Adilhayer's friends, as well as his wife and two relatives. My children were there, and so were my neighbors from the compound, who arrived with their relatives. Other guests included local businessmen and businesswomen and the principal and teachers of Maaly Art Academy, as well as staff from Agip KCO and other oil companies. Adilhayer couldn't believe that so many people had come to his exhibition to support him and his work.

As the ceremony began I started reading the speech I had written. I introduced the artist and spoke about his hard life, and how he'd dedicated his life to art. I thanked everyone who had worked with me on this project. I also thanked those who had come to see how this Kazakh artist expressed his particular vision of the world.

A year later I still remember this great experience in Kazakhstan. It showed me that if you take on a challenge and have faith, you will find a way to succeed. The Atyrau exhibition was only the beginning… at the moment I am preparing my next exhibition, this time in Milan and again in the company of my dear friend with the dark wild hair.

Winters in Astana

by Claire McCarthy

What do you do when the temperature drops below −20° Celsius? How can you live? Do you ever leave the house? What is there to do? These are the sorts of questions friends outside of Kazakhstan ask me. They can't imagine functioning in a place where you don't see the ground for up to three months of the year.

I spent my first Kazakh winter break enjoying the Australian summer. With its temperatures of 35° Celsius, I grew to enjoy pulling on a T-shirt and skirt and slipping into my flip-flops. On my return, alighting from the plane at 1 am into the freezing Astana night, dressed pretty much the same way, I realised I was going to have to change my attire. From then on, each morning would involve putting on the thermals my family had so kindly given me for Christmas, as well as my beaver fur hat, woollen mittens, fur boots and 50-year-old mink coat (kindly donated by my parents' neighbour).

Yet that first morning back in Astana, I awoke to discover the beauty that lay behind the freezing conditions. When the temperatures are so low, it seems that frost and blue sky cause everything to sparkle. After a relaxing day of getting over the long journey, I went out in the evening in an attempt to find my new gym (the address gave nothing away and it was unknown to every taxi driver I spoke to). I started to walk down my street towards the river and the park, where I was sure the gym would be. I soon found that there is plenty to do in Astana and that it is possible to escape from the house, even at temperatures of −52° Celsius!

Opposite my block of flats was a large building, which appeared to be some sort of educational establishment. The grounds were full of ice sculptures. Having been away for three weeks, I was not sure if they had been carved *in situ* or brought there. Either way, they were rather impressive. Continuing around the corner, I was met by the sight of a huge crowd. In the summer there were always lots of people going for their Sunday promenade along the river bank, but I had (wrongly) assumed that this would not be the case in deep mid-winter. People of all ages appeared to be throwing themselves down the river bank! Closer inspection revealed that slides had been built into the river bank. The walkway was lined with the old women who had sold popcorn and ice cream in the summer, now wrapped from head to toe in fur, and selling plastic sledges. All ages, from one to 90 were standing, sitting and lying about along the banks. I looked out across what had been the river and realised this was the place to be when you had free time. There were cross-country skiers, people on snowmobiles, others sledging or ice skating. Fishermen sat under tent-sized plastic bags, each with what looked like a large metal screwdriver (used to make a hole in the river) and a stool. They sat inside these bags waiting to catch fish (though considering the river is man-made, it was not clear to me what fish they would catch). I stood and watched the shivering fishermen for a while and then wandered through the park in the subzero temperatures, finally coming upon the gym.

On my way back, I came across another winter pastime in Astana… It seems that, to have a good time as a young male Kazakh, you all pile into a Lada and drive down to the riverside. You then drive at high speed along the frozen embankment until you come to a roundabout, where you pull a handbrake turn. The noise and resulting ice spray are really impressive but rather scary if you are walking alongside.

Another extreme ice sport I noted while walking through the park was snow-jogging. I am a keen jogger, but as I watched these guys turning blue in temperatures colder than a freezer, it seemed unnatural. They would jog past at a snail's pace and seemed to be deriving little pleasure from the exercise. I was just happy that I had found my gym and could wrap myself up in mink to get there.

By mid-February, the temperature still *way* below freezing (and set to stay that way for another month or so), and it was inevitable that one would be drawn towards any place that was warm. One Sunday afternoon, I decided to visit the city *banya* to warm myself up (and get clean in the process).

A *banya* is a form of steam bath. It was first heard of in Russia about 1,000 years ago and is similar to the Finnish sauna and Turkish hammam. It is basically a wooden hut, heated to temperatures above 90° Celsius, and there are various procedures to follow. I first discovered the joys of the *banya* back in the '90s, when I lived in Yaroslavl, a small city near Moscow, situated on the banks of the river Volga. On an early morning in mid-November, we dragged ourselves out of our warm beds, piled into our landlady's 1980s' Lada and set off for her house in the countryside, or *dacha*, to sample the private *banya*. On arriving at the village, I saw small wooden houses, each surrounded by a number of outhouses. As we were to discover, one of these was the bathing house. After a welcome vodka and some heavily salted fish, we were invited to enter the *banya*, which had been lit in preparation for our arrival and was now warm enough. Entering the small building, I was struck by the smell of newly cut grass and wet wood. We were told to strip off, wrap ourselves in a sheet and put on the felt hat given to us. We carefully entered the tiny, wooden room and were hit by a blast of scorching hot air. We sat on the wooden benches and started to slowly melt.

Shortly afterwards, a neighbour came in and gestured that I should go outside. I followed dutifully, thinking perhaps I would get a nice cool glass of water. I was mistaken. The woman took out a large bunch of birch leaves (*veniki*), told me to bend over and proceeded to beat the back of me furiously. The front side was, needless to say, even more painful. Once this was over I was sent outside and she duly threw a bucket of ice-cold water over me. I screamed at first, but then started to feel the blood rushing to my skin, which made me feel full of energy! Although the build-up wasn't particularly pleasant, the feeling afterwards was incredible. I went straight back in for another go at this amazing process. Reading up on the experience later, I found that it seems to have numerous health benefits, including an increase in heart activity leading to an increase of endorphins – something I was not surprised to hear.

Remembering my love of this Russian institution, I had searched out the Astana city *banya,* a five-storey building with male and female baths, to enjoy all those health benefits. In true Soviet style, there was a tiny cashier window at which to buy tickets and the obligatory employee stamping the entry tickets. I was given a sheet and flip-flops and I headed to the changing rooms. Inside were women of all ages, walking around with birch leaves (many also covered in the leaves) and carrying all kinds of toiletries.

I entered the hammam with hot stones first, where massages were being carried out, before moving on to the Finnish and

Turkish saunas and a large plunge pool. No one seemed to be using their leaves – until I entered the washroom. This was a huge hall with taps and bowls and showers, where women were scrubbing, cleaning, showering, chatting and, of course, slapping themselves with their birch leaves! After spending three hours of many rounds of the hot-and-cold treatment, I exited into the freezing early evening feeling warm. I was positively glowing.

By mid-March the temperatures in Astana hit the dizzy heights of 1° Celsius and, when the sun is shining, the city looks quite beautiful in places. During another of my walks through the park – and its complicated pathways – to the gym, I heard a swishing sound behind me, coming closer and closer. A man on skis shot past me, and I realised that I had wandered onto the ski track, which loops its way through the park. Despite having lived next to the mountains for two years in Almaty, I had little interest in skiing. My classroom had had a picture-perfect view of the snow-capped peaks and, although I was happy to look at them, I had never felt the need to go skiing (unlike my flatmate, who had regularly gone snowboarding). I did go up to the main ski resort on one occasion, purely to say I had visited it and to get some fresh air.

I had been skiing once, many years ago, when the dry ski slope first opened in Plymouth, England. I remember not enjoying it in the slightest! The next attempt was in Finland, where I spent the day cross-country skiing in Rovaniemi, in the Arctic Circle. As there were few slopes, I had enjoyed skiing through the fresh white countryside, watching the reindeer that roamed the forests.

The cross-country track in Astana's park piqued my curiosity and I decided to give it a go. I would take advantage of the blue sky and warmer temperatures to once more strap on a pair of skis. I found a ski rental shop in the big hotel in the park and, at £3 an hour to hire equipment, it seemed good value for money (and not too much to waste if I didn't enjoy the experience). Once I had hired the shoes and skis, I took them outside and placed the skis on the track. I then proceeded to spend the next 10 minutes trying to clip my shoes into the skis.

There were a number of people out on the track. They, of course, made it look simple (very much like people do when ice skating, another winter sport that I have never taken to!) I managed to eventually clip my shoes in, push off along the flat icy track, and promptly fall over. I am not clear on what causes one to lose balance when it is flat and you are not moving at great speed, but it happened a number of times, until I got used to the sensation of propelling myself along using the sticks and skis.

The course is kilometres long and is protected by trees, which helps you to forget that you are in the centre of a city. At the end of the hour, although I was cold and sore, I realised I had enjoyed myself. I felt I might have found a winter sport that I *was* able do! This discovery also added to my list of things one could do in the sub-zero winter temperatures of the second coldest capital in the world!

The Universal Language of Music

by Antonio Monreale

A song throws wide for you the world as open door,
A song floats dust to earth's own dust with mourning voice,
A song walks close at hand whenever we rejoice,
Pay every song due heed, and treasure it therefore.
– Abay Kunanbayuli, 19th-century Kazakh poet, composer
and philosopher

"You absolutely must come with us to the concert this evening," the internal communications officer said firmly.

It was the spring of 2006 in Atyrau, and I was on my monthly business trip to the city – an event I suspect was dreaded as much as loved by my colleagues, due to the hard work and long hours expected of us, as well as the continuous push for feedback and innovation. That night a traditional music concert was being sponsored by the company I worked for.

Young artists from the renowned Kazakh National Academy of Music in Astana would be performing, with traditional string instruments – such as the *dombra* and *kobyz* – and a variety of wind and percussion instruments making up the orchestra. Traditional Kazakh music has a rich history, and many of the melodies are treasures from nomadic oral folklore: epic and historical poems, fairytales and legends, proverbs and riddles that have been transferred from generation to generation… oral art, you might say.

The unexpected invitation appealed to me. I was reminded of my visits many years ago to the Barbican and the National Theatre festivals in London, that European city of multiculturalism, where I used to immerse myself in the music, enjoying the company of the eccentric habitués in the audience. I love music, and, despite a long and hard day, I felt I could not miss this experience.

Arriving at the Atyrau Drama Theatre, I was surprised to find no queue at the booking office. In about three minutes I was seated in the second row, next to my enthusiastic invitee, and the room began to fill up.

"X and Y did not come and hence you are the only senior manager in the audience," she said, then continued with a tranquil smile, "therefore you have to carry out the closing speech." Incredulous but trapped by duty, I had to accept the task as a token of appreciation for the invitation.

The concert lasted an hour. It was an intense experience, partly due to the heady music and partly due to my concern at having to make a speech without having done any preparation. During the concert I tried to find inspiration for my speech in the events around me: the orchestra's young and more senior members, the gestures of the conductor, the silence of the audience and the music itself. Melodic and soothing, then fast and rhythmic, then deep and solemn, the music led my emotions in a dance.

In the notes of the (to me, unfamiliar) traditional music, executed masterfully by the orchestra, I found fragments of familiar melodies and tunes. I was immediately struck by the idea that the music itself possibly contained, even was a code for, common human experiences and pursuits; that it might represent a set of universal emotions, a shared dignity and love.

I reflected on the diverse histories, cultures, origins and demographics of the audience, unexpectedly united that evening in that room, at that concert in Atyrau. I felt the powerful effect of the music on all of us. I observed the musicians, in their beautiful and colorful costumes, absorbed in their music sheets, yet alert to the gestures of the conductor. I watched them from the trepidation of the first note to the precision of the last, to the humble smiles at each round of applause. I realized that music is the simplest but highest expression of the human soul and spirit. Together with all the other arts, it embraces all cultures in a civilization often distracted by apparent differences, prejudices and daunting modern day life.

At the end of the show an interpreter accompanied me on stage, where a microphone was waiting for us. Pausing at intervals to give the interpreter time to translate, I told the audience where I was from and shared some of the reflections I had had during the concert. I shared the idea that artistic expression, and music in particular, spontaneously unites human experiences.

"Diverse cultures meet naturally through music with a common if mysterious understanding of it," I concluded after my stage companion's firm but kindly nod had signaled I should wrap up. I saluted the members of the orchestra and the conductor, and they silently moved through the back door of the stage in an orderly fashion. The interpreter descended the small steps just before me while the hall emptied. I was making my way down the steps when an elegant elderly man approached me, a smile on his face. After a short and polite exchange, the man spoke to me, slowly, in English.

"Thank you for this evening," he said. "I am content. When I was younger I was *akim* [mayor] for this region. Now I am an old man and you are all young and things are changing fast. My daughter works for your company, and I am very proud of that."

"Thank you," I replied with a warm handshake. I was as surprised and touched by that brief conversation as I had been by the evening that preceded it. The power of music had indeed brought people – and generations – together that evening. We were all reminded that it is the simple and spontaneous things that unite people.

Kazakh Legend on the Origin of Poetry and Music*

In ancient times none of the nations on the earth knew poetry and music. Life without poems was like a widow, life without music was barren. People did not laugh, holidays were not celebrated. Nature was sad and still: forests were silent, brooks didn't babble and birds didn't sing. At that time only the Heavens possessed the power of songs.

One day, a beautiful, mysterious and magical song decided to leave her home and explore the four corners of the Universe. Maybe she was tired of being of no use in the Heavens, maybe she just wanted to experience the wide steppe. Maybe she felt sorry for the Creation below and wanted to give it the gift of song, of delight and joy.

Depending on her mood, the song either flew low, or she shot upwards, high into an inaccessible sky. Those who were blessed with hearing her melodies and verses learned them by heart. Where she flew higher, people below heard only fragments. Some lands heard nothing at all … It is said that the song flew low over the Kazakh Steppe – and therein lies the secret to the richness of Kazakh poetry and music.

* Based on translation at http://musicheritage.nlrk.kz

Chapter 4

Cross-cultural Exchanges

Tea with Natasha

by Nina Buonaiuto

My teaching assistant, Irina, introduced me to Natasha one December day, and my husband and I hired her to be our housekeeper that same afternoon. Irina grew up with Natasha's daughter and has referred to Natasha as her second mother. I felt an instant bond with Natasha for reasons I can't really explain, other than to say she has a twinkle and a deep intelligence in her dark blue eyes. She shakes her head disapprovingly at my inability to clean the dirty rings off my husband's collar and yells at me to take off my shoes when I run through the house, something that would annoy me if it were anyone but her. I hate getting scolded in the playground for not dressing my three-year-old daughter, Sadie, warmly enough, but when it comes from her I recognise it as care rather than judgment.

I don't speak Russian and Natasha doesn't speak English. We use the few words we both know and fill in the spaces with gestures and pictures drawn on scraps of paper. Our conversations often end with giggles and resigned hand gestures of, "Okay, forget it." Sometimes she comes over with a new word. She offered the word 'friend' to Sadie the other day, in a gesture of goodwill that made Sadie look up briefly with recognition. She brought me the word 'learn' and attached it to the gesture of steering a car to explain that she is learning how to drive. But mostly we just talk in our own languages, hoping the other will understand anyway.

She brings Sadie a piece of candy every time she comes, and sometimes, small toys and trinkets. She has given us a pumpkin and homemade raspberry jam and brings us baked treats occasionally. Having her work for us is like having a really helpful mother around.

She invited us to have tea at her house last week. We walked there together with Sadie in the stroller. It only took 10 minutes, but as we crossed the street, we walked back in time to a different generation, a different country and culture, and into the life of a whole different breed of person. A hardier breed, knowledgeable in things I'm afraid my generation has lost, and exposed to a harder way of life.

Her neighborhood has potholes in the paved areas and mud puddles in the exposed dirt. The trees are older and greener than on my street and the people all move with that determined walk that suggests destination. The houses are mostly two-storey concrete and surrounded by tall fences and walls. I heard dogs barking and smelled coal fires. This neighborhood clings nervously onto a stretch of land that is being engulfed by the glittering new buildings of Astana. Across the street there are two, 30-foot-high televisions out of which glow the scenes of the modern age. Surrounding this old neighborhood are the bridges and super highways of a rapidly expanding capital city.

Natasha unlocked the heavy iron gate for us, and held back her barking dog while I quickly wheeled the stroller down a side path of her house to the backyard, glancing over my shoulder at the large, shaggy dog straining against her grip. Her backyard had several outbuildings and gardens. Dirt paths separated the areas of yard and were swept so clean even the rocks looked organized. The garden mounds were evenly spaced and ready for the fragrant tomato starts that were already growing in her hot house. The grape vines were trimmed and tied to a tall fence. Her cherry trees were in blossom and filled with droning bees. There was a skinny new apple tree, carefully protected under a tarp, and squash vines already snaking around the roots. The skyscrapers and city streets of Astana quickly ceased to exist in her backyard. We lingered outside naming things in Russian and English, while Sadie petted the mangy cat.

To get inside we climbed down a wooden set of narrow steps to a basement, where I recognized the boots that Natasha had worn to my house in the mud season, now carefully cleaned and sitting neatly side by side. Then we made a sharp left and climbed back up an even narrower set of steps, through a trapdoor, into the house. Natasha carried Sadie, happy for the excuse to hold her. Sadie is often very reserved around her, suspicious of her inability to understand what she is saying.

Her house was the indoor version of her yard and garden. Everything was old, but meticulously cared for and clean. The linoleum was a mismatched, old-fashioned pattern and her heavy, white enamel sink and taps looked antique. Everything that was old and frayed was carefully covered and mended. Everything that should have been stained with age was scrubbed clean. The antique-looking gas stove was a stark contrast to the electric range in my modern apartment. There was a peaceful feeling in her house, a feeling that people had really lived here and had appreciated and taken care of their possessions, a feeling of self-reliance. These are not people who buy things they don't need, or throw things away just because they're old. These are people that embodied the green lifestyle before it was ever born, or ever hip, in the Western world. I imagined her at night, carefully cleaning the kitchen and pruning her houseplants, mixing dough for pastries, squinting through her glasses as she sews. She is a busy woman, in constant motion, moving until she lies down to sleep. I thought about how we had hired this woman to clean for us and was conscious of how quickly the dynamics of our relationship had changed when I stepped into her house.

She offered us *blynys*, thin pancakes folded into triangles and arranged into a circular pattern on a plate. She poured homemade cherry jam into small, flowered, enamel bowls and demonstrated how to dip our *blynys* into it. Her dented electric kettle had the fabric wrapped cord I've seen on old appliances from my parent's generation. She poured us tea and carefully added cool water to Sadie's cup.

"I love tea at Natasha's house!" said Sadie, with her mouth full of *blynys* and cherry jam. I tried really hard to translate that accurately, with the arms crossed over chest, love symbol, and the word *chai* for tea and *dom* for house, some of the few words I know.

Without language, there was time to sit and observe in the comfortable silences that we shared. I marveled at her skills and the knowledge evident in the antique sewing machine and baskets of sewing tools, in her well-kept house and plants and perfect baked goods; evident too in the ceremony with which she made tea, making a really strong brew first and then adding hot water. I sat under the most perfect lemon tree I have ever seen, filled with lemons starting to ripen. I imagined the paths of our separate and very different lives, converging towards each other, towards this unusual and unlikely afternoon tea party.

She showed me pictures of her family and in gestures and a few words, I learned that she and her husband had met in Astana and had been married for 25 years. When they met she was a seamstress and he drove a train. Her husband had died of lung cancer, a month before I met her, a fact that I had learned from Irina, but had pretended not to know. She told me herself one day with the help of Google translator and gestures. It turned out to be his birthday that day, the day after Sadie's.

Sadie snooped around her house with the boldness of a three-year-old and managed to find the stuffed toy animals that once belonged to Natasha's now grown up daughters. She brought them all into the kitchen and lined them up on the floor to put them to sleep. I tried to explain to Natasha that after she leaves our house in the afternoon, Sadie rearranges her toys resentfully back on the floor where they were sleeping before Natasha cleaned them up. I wished I knew enough Russian to tell that her even though Sadie won't talk to her while she is at our house, she waits until she is sure she is gone, then opens the door and yells down the stairwell, "Bye Natasha, I still love you!"

Later, Sadie found some marbles in a bowl of shells. The shells were cleaned and arranged lovingly in a pattern. I thought about all the shells I've collected and forgotten about, realizing that her shells were probably from a hard-earned and treasured beach holiday. I wondered if I had appreciated my beach holidays enough, if I had really earned them. Sadie hid the marbles in her living room while we covered our eyes and counted, a trick she had just learned this year during Easter. We did that several times and then decided to go pet the cat one more time before we left. As we were getting ready, Natasha gave me a small houseplant to take home. She walked us down the road until she was sure we knew how to get home, even though I would have easily managed alone, then said goodbye.

I wondered why she had invited us. Does she feel the same connection to us that I feel towards her? Did she want me to see the extent of her full and rich life, to see her as more than a housekeeper, to understand her strength and capability? Did she think I didn't already know?

I wonder if she'll ever know how much it meant to me to be invited into her home. As an expat I often feel like an outsider trying to see in, but only able to see through the tinted lens of cultural assumptions. Does she feel this way when she comes to our home? Does she know this isn't really me? Overseas I live in borrowed apartments, never fully committed to people or places. After the thrill of a new country wears off, I find myself searching for the comfort and regularity of a normal life, which often means I stop trying to understand or belong. Seeing her home brought up that feeling in me again, the desire to settle, to find a less transient life, to know a community for many years. It made me want to grow my garden and put up my pictures and invite her to see my quiet life. But it also reawakened the desire to look deeper again, to understand different people and try harder to belong to this temporary life. In all my years overseas, this small, simple gesture was one of the more intimate and special occasions I've experienced. Walking into her kitchen, I realized, had felt like going home.

Birthdays and *Beshbarmak*

by Raquel Taravilla Pujado

The European project I was working on had been relocated to Atyrau and my family and I were looking forward to living in one of Kazakhstan's largest cities in the southwest of the country, very close to the Caspian Sea.

The company set us up in a hotel apartment in the city centre where we met lots of interesting people, including Zhanar, a friendly Kazakh woman, with long dark hair. In her mid-twenties Zhanar spoke perfect English and was studying for a chemistry degree in the United States. She was back in Kazakhstan to see family during her summer vacation. We had first started chatting to her in the hotel gym and she clearly felt comfortable in the company of Western expatriates. We got along so well that she invited us to her forthcoming birthday celebrations with her family and friends. We were slightly nervous about what to expect at a traditional Kazakh birthday party, but she was eager for us to join her and we were delighted to be invited, so we accepted immediately.

On the evening of the party our driver arrived to collect us and we travelled through the city centre to an old brown building, where Zhanar was waiting to greet us. We stepped inside a dark and dingy hallway and climbed up three flights of stairs to her apartment, where we removed our shoes in keeping with Muslim tradition (it is considered impolite to enter a clean home wearing outdoor shoes).

After introducing us to her family and friends, Zhanar invited us to sit around a table laden with exotic-looking food and adorned with golden decorations. Looking back,

I can't remember everything we ate because there was so much to choose from. I do remember the main course though: *beshbarmak*, a traditional Kazakh dish meaning 'five fingers' because it is eaten by hand. *Beshbarmak* is prepared with sliced boiled meat and onion, infused with spices and accompanied by noodles or pasta. Originally it would have been made with horsemeat but nowadays it can be made with different kinds of meats including camel, fish and chicken. Presented in a big round dish, large chunks of meat are dished up in bowls called *kese* and served with *shorpo*, a broth made from mutton.

Tradition states that a sheep's head is boiled in a *kazan*, a cauldron-style cooking pot, and then offered to the most distinguished or oldest guest, and in turn they carve the meat from the head, offering it to other guests around the table.

Depending on age and gender, party guests are offered different parts of the animal's carcass, with each bit being significant. The younger adults are usually given the leg and shoulder bones. Youths are given the sheep's ear with wishes to be careful and girls get the palate, in the hope that they will become good homemakers. Special guests are treated to gammon and shank; a young bride would be offered the brisket, and married women receive the neck-bones. Children are given the kidneys and heart, with the message that they are not yet mature, while knuckle is never served to a young girl because of the belief that she might remain an old maid forever. It was with some relief that we learned that the brain is always discarded because it is considered unsuitable to eat. An 'Amen' is always said at the end of a meal to give thanks to God.

On this occasion, we did not follow the *beshbarmak* ritual strictly to tradition and we were all given various parts of the sheep. We Westerners struggled to swallow, while trying to pretend it was delicious!

After nearly three hours of non-stop eating, numerous speeches, and mingling with Zhanar's relatives and friends, we were stuffed to bursting point, and naturally assumed the celebrations were drawing to a close when Zhanar's mother and sister began clearing the table. But as we stood up to thank our hosts, Zhanar asked if we would like to hear some traditional Kazakh pop music. Not wanting to offend the birthday girl, we headed off to her pretty bedroom with its floral décor to listen to her favourite tunes.

Half an hour later, Zhanar thanked us for coming to her party and said how pleased she was that we had been able to make it. We felt sure the celebrations were winding down as we began to make our way to the front door. But just as we started putting our shoes on, Zhanar's mother and sister began laying out more food on the tables.

Despite our protestations about feeling full-up and that we had to get up for work in the morning, Zhanar's family cheerfully ignored our excuses and good-naturedly insisted we continue the celebrations and carry on eating! I desperately wished that I had paced myself earlier because I had no idea how I could possibly consume anything else.

Finally, another hour and a half later, the party was drawing to a close and we thanked Zhanar and her family for their generous hospitality. As we waddled sleepily to our car, we reminisced about the wonderful evening we had had, and how fortunate we were to have experienced a traditional Kazakh birthday party.

Drinking Camel's Milk in the Yurt

by Monica Neboli

"My mother would be really happy to have you and the girls as our guests tomorrow for lunch." Sholpan, our dear Kazakh friend, was calling to invite us to visit her parents in their village; my husband, unfortunately, was attending a conference on the other side of the world.

We first met Sholpan when we arrived in Kazakhstan two years ago. At the time Sholpan was a teacher in the local school in Atyrau and she wanted to improve her English by working with an expat family, in the hopes of being hired by the QSI International School of Atyrau. Within two years, showing characteristic Kazakh determination, Sholpan had passed from the role of nanny to my youngest daughter, Agata, to that of teacher's assistant in the class of my eldest, Eleonora, at the international school.

"Monica, are you still there?"

I had been daydreaming about our visit.

"Yes, sure, it will be our pleasure," I replied.

Sholpan had told us a lot about Damba, a fishing village of about 3,000 souls in the suburbs of Atyrau, and her birthplace. Her parents still lived there and it was an unfailing source of tales, anecdotes and superstitions, all of which Sholpan would describe to us in great detail.

I remember in particular the stories she told us about the phantoms roaming her village. Nobody in the village had seen them, but everyone knew it was best not to encounter them.

"The young guys of the village who had seen a phantom while coming home late at night had either disappeared forever or lost their minds," she had told us with a serious expression.

The tales always brought great excitement for our daughters, though the consequence was often a sleepless night for my husband and I, who were forced to share our bed with two kids who would take fright at the slightest noise.

On the morning of our visit to Damba, there was a joyful atmosphere in our house. My daughters were eager to meet the parents of their friend. While I was dressing them, I tried to mentally recap the little information I had learnt in the past two years on Kazakh etiquette for guests: never arrive without a present; never use the left hand to eat; and at the end of the meal, always remember to thank your host with the *amin*, a Muslim gesture of thanks that involves cupping the hands and passing them down the face.

The company's minibus, which we were not allowed to drive ourselves, arrived to take us to the village and would wait there for our return. Leaving Atyrau city, which sits along the Ural River, my daughters became captivated by the landscape of the steppe. We entertained ourselves by attempting to spot the various animals grazing quietly along the riverside and on the plains: wild horses, camels and cows, and those small, funny brown animals, the souslik (or ground squirrel), which would appear unexpectedly here and there behind the bushes, before disappearing just as quickly a few seconds later. I was always the last to spot them in our games.

Along the river I caught a glimpse of small, green open spaces, ideal for spring picnics, during which – as the Kazakh tradition dictates – *shashlyk* would be served: skewered pieces of meat cooked on the grill. These have become, for the expat community too, a delicious tradition.

Along the road, the small houses, even if simple and still under construction, were on the whole more attractive than the buildings we had left behind in the city. Each dwelling was surrounded by a small garden, often with flowers and plants.

When we arrived in Damba, Sholpan's mother opened the minibus door and welcomed us with a beaming smile, making us feel immediately at home. Like Sholpan, both parents had Asiatic traits, with those beautiful black eyes common especially to Kazakhs. Sholpan's father, who was more reserved, was waiting for us behind the fence. Neither of her parents spoke English so Sholpan was our official translator for the day.

The family led us directly to see the new house that Sholpan, with the savings from her job at the international school, was building for her parents. Only the walls had been completed at this stage, but it was going to be beautiful: two floors, bedrooms for the whole family and a big, cheerful kitchen. The only flaw, alas, was the bathroom. Although toilets are generally found outside the Kazakh home, there was no sewer system in the village, so the family had to make do with what they had: a big hole dug in the garden, around which they had built a small concrete cabin.

The little cabin, outwardly so nice, was a great source of interest for my daughters. They amused themselves by running around it while the adults explored the new house, until Agata called, "*Mama*, I need to pee."

When she saw the hole inside the "dolls' house" she began to cry. After about 10 minutes of trying to convince her to use the toilet, we had to find a spot for her to pee in the garden.

A step or two away was another house, smaller than the one under construction, which was the family's home in the mean time. We moved towards the entrance, the neighbours curiously watching these expats visiting their village. At the entrance we took off our shoes. This was a habit that we had already become accustomed to in Egypt, our previous destination as expatriates. The house had a small entrance; there was a kitchen to the right and in front was a room with a low table in the centre. On the floor around the table were carpets traditionally used in yurts. Along two sides of the room were two modern *kebezhe*, small wooden pieces of furniture decorated with Kazakh symbols. On top of these, thick coloured quilts were piled high.

Sholpan's mother invited us to take a seat on the floor. It was devilishly hot and the rooms were full of gadflies. The house was in semi-darkness; on the windows were heavy, colourful curtains, slightly open so only a few glimmers could filter in. Sholpan's father, sitting on the sofa in the living room next door, was watching television. My daughters began to run around the room, jumping up and down on the couch. It was unusual behaviour for them, but the man was laughing and playing with them, so I let it continue. Within a few seconds Agata was sitting in his lap, calling him *nonno* (Italian for grandpa) and stroking his face.

In the meantime, I headed with my friend to the kitchen, a small room with a fire stove and a table, and a refrigerator on the other side of the door. Washing up was done outside the house in water poured into big basins. Sholpan began to wash the glasses that were on the table and then passed them to me to set the table for lunch. While Sholpan's mother was finishing the cooking, we then put the coloured quilts on the floor around the table in the dining room. The girls soon arrived, hungry and curious to try new flavours. A little later our minibus driver appeared; he had been invited for lunch by Sholpan's parents. We sat down on the quilts and each diner received a cup of chai and a bowl of broth.

Sholpan's mother soon entered with a steaming dish of *beshbarmak*, the most famous and traditional of Kazakh meals. As we began to eat, I felt proud of my daughters, who were eating their meal with their hands without batting an eye. They were sharing in the joy and fun of lunch with our companions. They already felt part of this world, and part of this family who were hosting us so warmly.

We finished the lunch with an *amin* and Sholpan suggested we visit the village. My daughters agreed immediately – they looked forward to running among the houses. The day was fantastic, warm and dry, and we headed towards the Ural River. The houses were positioned along parallel lines between the river and the main road. We were walking on hard mud, the same mud that, during the rainy days, sticks to your boots and is so difficult to remove when it has dried.

On arrival at the river bank, we noticed a yurt in front of us. It was not the kind of yurt that we were used to seeing during Nauryz. (During this celebration, the main square of Atyrau is full of yurts covered by white sheets on which typical Kazakh symbols are painted in blue and red.) This yurt appeared more traditional: it was covered by felt carpets bound together with ropes whose ends were knotted around stones positioned around the yurt. The small wooden door, which in Kazakh tradition looks to the south, was inlaid with purple geometric drawings.

Sholpan knocked at the door and said something in Kazakh. An old woman opened the door. She had on a sky blue hat and her face was a web of wrinkles on amber skin. She looked at us with a warm smile and I understood that she had been waiting for us. We left our shoes outside and entered the yurt.

As we grew used to the dim light, we saw a cosy interior, which was surprisingly cool. We walked across felt carpets in red and white, while yet more carpets covered the walls and part of the ceiling. We sat down on a sofa near a low table. Eleonora and Agata, enchanted by the charm of this new kind of tent, were strangely calm as they sat by my side.

After exchanging a few words with Sholpan, the old woman walked across to a beautiful *kebezhe*, above which a goatskin hung. She filled some glasses and offered them to us. Sholpan explained that the glasses held camel's milk, a delicious, nutrient-rich drink considered important for the health of young and old in Kazakhstan. I overcame the temptation to guzzle it down when I saw my daughters and Sholpan sipping at it politely.

While slowly drinking my milk, which was saltier than cow's milk, my eyes were drawn to the blue sky, which peeped through the hole at the top of the yurt. I was surrounded by a feeling of peace and serenity. I felt completely in tune with this land, which had welcomed me for the past two years. I felt so happy to add this experience to my life's memories and so lucky to have the opportunity to get to know the Kazakh traditions in a deeper way. Even today I carry that feeling with me, as I do the taste of that glass of camel's milk, which I drank slowly to savour every last drop.

Table of Unity

by Gualtiero Bestetti

It was a Friday evening in Atyrau. The outside temperature was –27° Celsius. Everything was frozen: the river, the trees… it was surreal. That night we had a dinner appointment with our landlord – our first invitation from a local since we had moved here.

We had come to Atyrau a year ago with our little boy, who was nearly two years old at the time. We had decided not to live in a compound but in a Kazakh building, so we could live among locals and feel at home, rather than as if we were living in a hotel. It was difficult in the beginning because of the language barrier, but our location was fantastic. We were in a large building by the river and it had a playground in the courtyard, where children would play in summer (and sometimes in winter). We were the first foreigners to move into the building and our neighbours, who were polite and tried to speak a few words in English, seemed happy to have expatriates in the building. It was particularly special for us to see our son playing with Kazakh children in the playground, in spite of their cultural differences. Children speak a universal language; they don't care about differences. There is a lot we can learn from them.

We had deliberated on how to dress for the evening ahead, what sort of wine to bring and which Italian dessert to prepare. Our landlord would be collecting us and then we would go together in his car, as company security policy did not allow us to drive ourselves. The doorbell rang.

"Hallo?" said my wife.

"Allo?" a man's voice answered.

"Hallo?" my wife repeated.

"Allo?" the voice said again. "Arianna?"

"Yes, I'm Arianna. But who are *you*?"

"I'm Andrej."

We had just learned a rather quirky cultural difference: when you ring someone's bell here, you do not say, "Hi, it's…" Instead you say the name of the person you are calling on, and they have to guess who you are.

We wrapped ourselves up: winter boots, gloves, scarves, a mink hat bought at the local market just to feel like we were one of them. But not being locals, we hadn't been prepared for this diabolical cold!

We walked downstairs and a huge car was waiting for us.

"Lexus," said my son, who knows every make of car.

"*Zdrastvuite Andrej,*" we chorused. ["Hello Andrej."]

"*Zdrastvuite Andrej,*" repeated our son as we stepped into the car, whose seats were covered with fur. After 10 minutes driving around streets covered with ice and mud, we arrived at a huge three-storey house on the river, with a beautiful garden – in stark contrast to the streets just outside their door, which had felt like no man's land.

The men shook hands (never with the women) as we took off jackets, gloves, scarves and hats and were led inside. The house was vibrant, with splashes of colour everywhere… on the floor, the wallpaper, the sofa. We were shown the fitness room with its small pool and sauna. The enormous living room was decorated in black and gold. In the kitchen – red, with two family-sized fridges – we found our hostess, who was preparing dinner. We had brought a special Italian dessert, known as chocolate salami, which we put in the fridge.

We went up wide wooden stairs to another huge, colorful living room, with pictures on the walls. A table, for 20 or more, was laden with starters and desserts: a tomato and pickle salad, fruit salad, sweets, dried plums, nuts, grapes, tea with milk, a variety of juices, cake... The main dish – *manti*, a sort of steamed ravioli filled with mutton and my favourite Kazakh food – was later served by our hostess.

We felt shy in all this solemnity, but we understood that we were the first foreign guests in their home and that they were proud to entertain us. We were shortly introduced to the Kazakh tradition of making a toast, which is something of a ceremony here. The eldest man, or a special guest, has to manage the sequence of toasts, for every man at the table must say one (women do not toast). I've never enjoyed making toasts, as my team at work quickly learned. (At my farewell party, nobody said a toast or asked me to say one. However, before I left, made a touching 'personal toast' to me.) Kazakh people *love* to make toasts. For them, every moment is a good moment for a toast. Our landlord did his half in English and half in Kazakh.

"Thank you to my Italian friends. I'm so happy to have you in our house and to enjoy this food with you. I wish you, your family and your children all the best. I hope you enjoy your stay in Kazakhstan."

Soon it was my turn and, despite my embarrassment, I managed to express our gratitude for this special experience.

We have lost this sense of solemnity in what we do, I reflected later. Our hosts had also reminded us of the importance of respect and a love for simple things.

A few months later, we decided to invite these same Kazakh friends for dinner, as they had been asking for a typical Italian meal.

"Great!" said my wife, who loves to entertain at our home.

That Saturday morning we headed out to the supermarket, where we bought wine for the starter, as well as a red wine for the main course and a sweet wine for the dessert. We had decided on the following menu: tomato *bruschette* (slices of toasted bread covered with garlic and tomato) and Italian salami, lasagne, and home-made *crostata* (a baked dessert often with jam filling).

Later, my wife was finishing preparing the *bruschette* when the bell rang.

"They are here!" I called.

Our guests looked disappointed when they saw the table empty of food. Silence reigned in the kitchen, so I quickly poured the Prosecco to make a toast (of course!). I don't think they liked it much – it is very different from vodka! My wife then explained that dinner would be composed of three courses and that each would be paired with a special wine. They were excited to try everything we served, although so shy at the beginning that I believe they hardly tasted the food.

My wife's "Lasagne's ready!" was met with happy faces, for they knew and liked lasagne. We changed glasses and I poured the best red wine I had been able to find. Slowly our guests started to appreciate the meal, asking for more lasagne – and for more wine! They were especially curious about Italian wines, asking how there came to be such a variety of wines in Italy and how wine is produced. By the end of the evening, they were enjoying themselves and all shyness had worn off.

Like the dinner at their home, this was a wonderful cross-cultural experience we will never forget.

Fun and Games at a Kazakh Birthday Party

by Tolga & Ozlem Tekiroglu

It was a summer's evening in Atyrau, the temperature sitting at 40° Celsius, and I was running late. My family was back in our home country, Turkey, and I had been invited by one of my Kazakh employees to the 55th birthday party of his mother. I had heard that he had received a loan from the bank to fund the celebrations. While waiting for the lift, I heard, "Help, help!"

The lift was out of order and someone was stuck inside it! We lived in an apartment that had been advertised with photos of "a beautiful panorama of the city". When we had moved in though, we had found that the inside of the building told quite a different story: the heating system was poor, the house-keeping left something to be desired, water and electricity were often cut off, and the furniture was old. Not to mention that we were in a fourth-floor apartment and the lift was frequently out of order.

I immediately ran over to the maintenance office in the building next door. They were always quick to respond to any problems in our building. I knocked on their door and quickly told them what had happened.

"Okay, no problem," the two men calmly replied. "As you can see, we are eating dinner. We'll rescue them when we're done."

Astonished, I went back to the lift and, hiding my concern, I explained that the maintenance guys would come as soon as they had finished working on "another technical hitch". As I couldn't do much more, I made my way to the party. Twenty minutes later I was running towards the restaurant entrance thinking I was terribly late. Fortunately, the guests were still standing about. I learned that night that a start time is just an approximation and that events may even start a couple of hours late. The risk then is to arrive *on time* and not find anyone else there!

There were probably about 150 people at the party, of which I was the only foreigner. The men mostly wore dark suits, while the women floated about in various colored dresses (and some very high heels). The tables were laden with different salads, vegetables and meats, as well as a selection of small cakes and candies placed on a cake stand. The presentation of the meal in all its variety and color was striking. Waiters walked about, serving alcoholic drinks and small glasses of vodka.

Galim, my employee, immediately came over to give me a warm welcome and to introduce me to his mother, the guest of honor, a small, smiling woman wearing a dark red traditional Kazakh dress. Galim then introduced me to the other guests at my table.

The dining began, along with speeches by family members and close friends of the birthday girl, each speech accompanied by vodka and a toast. When it was my turn to toast (as each guest must do at a traditional Kazakh social event), I did not speak in Turkish or English, as expected, but rather in my rather rudimentary Kazakh, using a few special words for wedding toasts that I had memorized. The group appreciated my attempt and laughed, obviously pleased with the gesture. I was rather proud of myself, but my sense of accomplishment was not to last!

I thought we were finished eating, but I soon discovered that the food on the table had been only the starter. Waiters were now bringing out *beshbarmak* (literally meaning 'five fingers'), a traditional Kazakh meal made with horse and lamb's meat. The *beshbarmak* was served in big round dishes and, as the name suggests, eaten using the hands. Finally we were served tea, cakes and fruits.

The evening continued with eating, dancing, shows, games and various competitions (and more toasts), though I preferred to watch rather than participate. Just as I was finally starting to relax after the dramatic start to my evening, I was chosen for a new game, along with three other guests. The foreigner at the party was not going to be allowed to sit out!

Okay, let me get it over with, I thought.

The Master of Ceremonies summoned us to choose, without looking, from various traditional attire from around the world. We were then told to don our suits and dance accordingly. Mine was from Africa. While dancing in as much African style as I could muster, I imagined my wife and children watching and laughing themselves silly. I went from workdays in a formal suit with tie to African dress and dancing in front of 150 people at my employee's mother's birthday party! It was the hardest five minutes of any birthday party I've ever been to – especially because my moves were being recorded on every mobile phone or camera present. That was the last time I took part in any games at Kazakh parties!

When I returned home later that night, I remembered the poor souls stranded in the lift. Were they still imprisoned inside it, or had their rescuers finally found the time to release them? To my relief, the lift was empty... and none of us used it again.

Chapter 5

Travelling in Kazakhstan

On the Road Without a GPS

by Olga Jaworska

My biggest dream was about to come true: my parents, sister and I were planning a trip to southern Kazakhstan. I started counting down the days to the summer break and spent hours looking at a huge map of Kazakhstan on the wall of my bedroom in Astana. I found pictures of the Aral Sea and watched it disappearing due to past Soviet irrigation projects. I knew the names of all the towns of the region by heart. I was close to reciting the data of their population sizes. Then we realized there was no road connecting Aralsk and Aktau. This fact was confirmed by friends of my parents who had gone on a month-long trek from Astana to Aktau and back. Without tents, more time, and an off-road car with a huge trunk, the trip would remain just a dream. So, that same summer we took two separate trips around the country instead: one eastwards to the Altay mountains close to the border with China, and the other to the south (Almaty, Taraz and Turkestan) and on to Kyrgyzstan. It is the first that I want to tell you about…

Kazakhstan did not disappoint us and my desire for adventure was almost fulfilled. On our journey we realized that maps can never completely reflect the reality (especially as they aren't constantly updated with satellite photos). In fact, our *three* maps of the same area made it even harder for us to move around. How do you decide where to turn when one map shows an intersection after a village, the second hints at a turn before the village, and the third doesn't acknowledge the presence of either the village or the road?

And don't be surprised when a trip you planned takes two days instead of one – because of the poor quality roads that don't even exist according to one map, and are considered the best by another. All these difficulties (and detours) are allowed for by the low price of gas – *if* there is a gas station that sells good-quality fuel nearby, and provided their electricity is working when you arrive.

In spite of having spent her childhood in the Polish countryside, my mom was close to losing her mind a few times during the trip, as we were exposed to the peculiarities of village life in Kazakhstan. In an Altay village of Urunkhayka, where the temperature on a summer evening is slightly above zero, we stopped to look for a place to spend the night. We had been told that the locals were prepared for tourists and that finding a night's lodging would be fairly easy. However, it proved to be anything but, and it was starting to get late. My mom's desperation was growing, and the rest of us weren't especially excited at the prospect of staying in the car for the next few hours.

While we were driving around the village asking the locals for a guesthouse or a hotel, a young woman walking towards us said we could rent a room at her place in about half an hour, after she had led her cows home. We were still surprisingly optimistic about finding an alternative and told her we would return if we weren't successful.

Later we bumped into a group of teenagers listening to music on a mobile phone and stopped to ask them where we could find a guesthouse.

"I think there is a hotel over there," one of the teenagers replied in Russian. "They might have a room for you."

What are you saying?" replied another. "You call that tiny house that is about to fall apart a hotel?"

It was our only option we were told. The only guesthouse in the village was under construction and a lady who usually rented out rooms had gone "to the city" – the city being half a day's drive away. After driving up a hill we found the 'hotel'; a house that looked like every other house in the village. The owner, it turned out, was the cattle-herding woman we had met as we had entered the village.

We agreed to her price, although it was pretty high considering the conditions, because we didn't want to spend the night in the car. We unloaded the most important items from the car and stepped inside the house. It was too dark to look around properly, but we were too tired to care. We soon discovered that, although the rest of the house had electricity, the sole light bulb in our bedroom didn't work. We accepted this with a few groans and changed into our pajamas in complete darkness. I lay down on the uncomfortable bed, feeling the chill through drafty windows, and couldn't fall asleep because of the noise of a television, and our host conversing in Kazakh on a cell phone.

In the morning, when the absence of electric light was no longer a problem, we had a breakfast composed of our own food supplies and the hostess's boiled water for tea. After coming through some minor trouble, most notably learning to use the host's kettle and opening a glass of processed cheese by mistake, we set out in the direction of Lake Markakol. We didn't intend to swim, but we expected to at least be able to feel the temperature of the water with our fingers. Again, our dreams were crushed by the reality of the Kazakh countryside. The water was crystal clear and home to some interesting wildlife… We weren't able to get out of our car thanks to a bull that was sauntering towards us. We consoled ourselves with a few photos and drove away.

After a few kilometers, we noticed that the meadows had changed color, from green to yellow-orange. We left the car equipped with three cameras. On closer inspection, the meadows proved to be even more beautiful than we had thought, and my parents compared it to those postcard views of the Alps. My mom, a proud gardener, ran about the meadow taking pictures of every type of flower, bush and grass. Today, we still remember this moment as one of the happiest of our travels in Kazakhstan.

"Why did she have weeds in her garden if she could dig some flowers from that meadow?" my mom wondered later, referring to our hostess from the previous night. I didn't feel like explaining that the meadow seemed nearby only to us, with our 4x4 and plenty of time on our hands.

I quickly forgot about our sleepless night in the village as we drove through the breathtaking variety of Kazakh landscapes: mountains, deserts, and steppes. We had to concentrate on the potholes in the road, as well as the road signs and our infamous maps, so there was little time to contemplate the daily lives of the people we encountered.

The next moment of confusion came a few hours later, when we were required to turn from the main road in the direction of the town of Zaisan. We took a guess, turned and drove about 15 kilometers – almost off-road – onto the steppe. We came to a village and saw that the only exit was the road on which we had entered. We asked a man on horseback for directions.

"I don't know," he said in broken Russian. He pointed at one of the houses near us, suggesting its owner would be able to help. An old man, who was sitting on a bench in front of the house, told us how to return to the main road. As we were leaving the village, I heard the sound of something falling to the ground, but thought it was our luggage in the trunk shifting as we drove on the uneven road. We continued on our way back to the main road.

By this stage we needed fuel desperately, and only some unknown miracle saved us from spending a few days in the cold desert. (We drove on reserve, which had been due to run out about an hour before we hit the first gas station.) Shortly after refueling, my dad discovered a malfunction in the car. Fortunately, the problem wasn't serious and he was able to fix it himself, using pieces of junk he found at the gas station. It was while doing this that he noticed our back number plate was missing. I immediately thought of the sound I had heard that morning, in the no-name village on the steppe. It was too late to go back now, so we decided to worry about it later. Our priority was rather to find a place to spend the night, which was quickly approaching.

We found a hotel in Ayagoz, a town in the southern part of eastern Kazakhstan. We were happy to have a warm, weatherproof place to stay as the town welcomed us with a storm. Once settled in, we took one of our maps and made a provisional number plate using a marker and a red pencil we found in my sister's pencil case. This plate was replaced twice by other better-looking makeshift plates after our journey, and we are still in the process of getting a proper one.

After Ayagoz, we spent another day driving to Karagandy, on a road that was marked red on all our maps, but was nevertheless impassable in places. We knew there was no chance of getting to Astana before night so we decided to head for the Karkaraly National Park. After confusing the names Karkaraly and Karagaily, which resulted in another detour, we found our way to the park. The owner of the first hotel we found was stunned when we requested a room.

Are you crazy? his expression said.

"We don't have running water or electricity," he explained, "but you can stay in a unit with windows." Then he thought again and recommended a better hotel nearby. "All the tourists stay at Shakhtyor," he said.

The hotel was easy to find and we concluded that it must indeed be popular to get away with charging those sorts of prices. We ended up in another guesthouse for the night and looked forward to spending the morning in the mountain forest nearby. It turned out that the only way to the mountain trails led through Shakhtyor's territory and that the hotel's security charged for entering. Fortunately, our host told us about a hole in the fence that all her guests use to access the mountains. We did the same and didn't have any problems, even when we did bump into the guards. We enjoyed a morning hike, collected a large bouquet of wild flowers, and then headed for home. We arrived in Astana a few hours later – remarkably, without incident.

There we started packing for our next journey. But that's a different story…

Tales of a Traveling Teacher

by Linda van de Sande

"Twenty years from now you will be more disappointed by the things you didn't do than by the ones you did do. So throw off the bowlines. Sail away from the safe harbor. Catch the trade winds in your sails. Explore. Dream. Discover." – **Mark Twain**

In August 2011, I threw off the bowlines, flew away from the safety of my home in Belgium, and caught the Atyrau wind to the QSI International School of Atyrau. I explored, dreamed and discovered... Friends and family wondered why I had picked Kazakhstan, known to many of us only as the country from the Borat movies, as my next destination. Many of us didn't even know where it was located. But the not knowing would be part of the adventure and the highlight of my stay would be my travels, which I did by train... just like a modern-day Kazakh nomad.

It was October, fall break. I had been here for two months and was ready for a short vacation. In Atyrau we don't have trees, not unless you count the purple and yellow plastic trees along the streets that light up in the evening. There is no grass or mountains either, so the city is flat and sandy. I decided to travel to Turkestan, one of the pilgrimage sites in Kazakhstan, a city that lies between Kyzylorda and Shymkent on the famous Silk Road.

Five colleagues and I started our journey at Atyrau's train station. The trip to Turkestan was to take around 33 hours. Our carriage was perfect for six people: three beds on one side and three bunk beds on the other. The beds turned into seats during the day and in the middle of the carriage was a small table. It was an open carriage, which meant we could see our neighbouring passengers – a great opportunity to make friends! The train had one dining car where you could drink chai and eat delicious *kespe* (homemade noodles) and *borsh*, a soup with meat and noodles. Most passengers however, bring their own food and that's what we did: plastic plates, cups, utensils, coffee, tea, bread, rice; we were prepared for our journey.

The train stopped in every big town along the way. People got off to buy food or drinks, to smoke or just to stretch their legs. We arrived in Turkestan at 2 am. We hadn't booked a hotel – nomads don't do that! – and ended up at a market, very sleepy after the long ride. The only help we had was a travel guide book and Sholpan, one of our colleagues. If you thought that the Turkestan market is quiet at 2 am then you'd be quite wrong! Some of the vendors were sleeping in their shops, but others were getting ready for the next day. We asked about hotels or places to sleep. The market's security guards were friendly and helpful, but unfortunately all the rooms at their recommended spot were occupied. Eventually, with the help of our guide book, we found a hotel near the mausoleum.

The next morning, or rather, a few hours later, we awoke and decided to walk around the city. We had breakfast in a local restaurant, which was a series of rooms, each with tables and chairs. Coffee, tea and food were cheap in Turkestan compared to the oil city of Atyrau. I particularly enjoyed my Russian *plov* (a meat dish with rice and carrots that resembles Uzbek *palau*)!

In the afternoon we visited the Mausoleum of Khodja Akhmed Yassaui, which thoroughly deserves its place on the list of UNESCO World Heritage sites. The walls were adorned with blue and turquoise tiles. Above the mausoleum was a ribbed turquoise dome, decorated with geometrical designs. No wonder we saw so many newly-weds, for the mausoleum was the perfect backdrop for wedding pictures. While walking around, we met an old man who was a professional *dombra* player. (A *dombra* is a two-stringed wooden Kazakh guitar.) He sang for us and signed the *dombras* we had bought earlier in the journey.

The next day we went to the big bazaar in the center of Turkestan. We took a local bus, which are usually small and crowded, with standing room only (unless you sit on someone's lap). Luckily it was not far to the bazaar. Inside the bazaar, we found: scarves, socks, clothes and an array of souvenirs. Outside the bazaar, people were selling colourful, shiny fruit and vegetables. The carrots in Turkestan are bright orange and the tomatoes are the best I have ever had.

Soon it was time to take the train again, this time to Tulkubas, a small town near the Aksu Zhabagly Nature Reserve. Zhabagly is a farming village of around 2,000 people. We had booked a guesthouse in the mountains, so that we could enjoy Kazakh nature during the last days of our trip. The guesthouse was owned by a couple, a Dutchman called Lammert and Elmira, his Kazakh wife of 20 years. They wanted to share their love of nature with tourists escaping the busy cities. Lammert picked us up from the train station and we arrived at the guesthouse to a warm welcome; we immediately felt at home. Breakfast was ready when we arrived, and after we had finished, Elmira asked if we wanted to hike in the mountains. Of course we did! She made up a packed lunch for us and we took the bus into the mountains. The weather was perfect: the sun was shining and the temperature was around 20° Celsius. We hiked until we reached some waterfalls. We didn't see any other tourists, only some local men on horseback, and it was a luxury to have the mountains and the gorgeous scenery all to ourselves. After a typical 'crazy jump' picture, we headed back to relax in the self-made sauna: a small room with a fire inside. After a mud bath, with black mud from the mountains, it was time for a walk in the village.

One of the things I like most about traveling is interacting with locals. Even if you don't speak the language, there's always a way to communicate. We ended up chatting with a carrot farmer, who was cleaning some carrots and roasting a sheep's head. (Sheep – and horse – feature regularly on a Kazakh menu, especially at parties.)

It was hard to leave this sanctuary, but we had to go back to our life in Atyrau, back to reality… This time we boarded an old Soviet coal train, which was much slower than our original train to Turkestan and had windows that didn't open. On board we met an old drunk, a Russian, who brought vodka and some smelly fish to our carriage. We told him that we were allergic to fish, so he removed it, but returned with music. He was in the mood for a party! After a while though he got the message that we didn't really like his party, and he left. We made friends with Sasha the conductor too, and watched as he added coals to boil water. He felt almost fatherly as he took care of this group of foreigners on his train.

It's unusual for expats to travel by train, but it's an experience I recommend. I enjoyed every moment of our journey. I would fall asleep to the sound and movement of the train and wake up to see the sun rising over the steppe. We watched camels and wild horses along the way and grew accustomed to the blue-

and-white painted houses that feature in every village. The trip was also a wonderful introduction to the Kazakh culture, and after a week spent surrounded by nature, I had enough energy to work until the next vacation!

Chapter 6

The Silent Steppe

Dirt Roads, a Donkey and a Life Transformed

by Victoria Charbonneau

I have always had a place in my heart for unwanted children. Through the miracle of adoption, I am a single mom to two US-born bi-racial children. As a little girl, I dreamed of living on a large farm filled with children and animals. Being an artist I dreamed in full color; I envisioned children from many different ethnic groups learning about life through gardening, animals and farm activities.

Due to many detours in life, that dream had been shelved – until I heard about a group helping to put on a camp for orphaned children in Kazakhstan. I attended their presentation and, crazy as it seemed, I knew in my heart that I had to go. The faces of the children on the screen were the same ones I had dreamed of as a little girl. My decision led to an 18-day trip that changed the course of my life.

As I boarded the plane in October 2000, I was all of a sudden filled with panic. What was I doing? Why was I leaving my own precious kids to go halfway around the world? I didn't know anything about the land of Kazakhstan. What had I agreed to? After what seemed like days of travel, the plane landed in the middle of the night. Things had surely improved since Kazakhstan's independence, but the old airport in Almaty was so different from anything I had ever seen on my limited travels around the US.

I stepped off the plane and onto the tarmac. Military personnel stood with large guns. But my most vivid memory of that night is of looking up into the vast sky and seeing millions of twinkling lights shining upon us. Emotion flooded my heart as a gentle breeze blew across my face. I was home, in a land where I belonged. I was surprised by this feeling. The unfamiliar smells, the sight of armed men, and the sounds of an unknown language did nothing to take away that feeling of being in a place I had long been missing. The seeds of love for Kazakhstan in all its majestic beauty and contradictions were planted that night.

As we headed to the orphanage, I was beyond tired. I was hungry and aching from head to toe. Fortunately, the majestic mountains and sweeping views of the steppes kept my excitement alive. After a grueling 10-hour ride in a van loaded up with passengers and supplies, we pulled into the Ulan Orphanage in Taraz. As we rounded the corner, we were greeted by more than 150 children standing out in that cold spring day, waving and cheering as we came to a stop. I stepped out of the van, my weariness leaving me as I was greeted by smiling faces. I shook the children's cold hands and my heart melted and was captured forever.

Every human has a desire for their life to matter, their story to be known. I could tell you stories about so many of the children, but this story is about Oldana, a waif of a teenage girl with a big smile and a love of dancing. Her graceful movements were in stark contrast to the sadness in her eyes. She was shy and hung back, unlike most of the children who pushed and shoved to be near the Americans.

By 2009, I had relocated to Kazakhstan to live and work with the children. My own children were adults by this stage. I wanted to do what I could to assist the caregivers in preparing their Kazakh charges for life outside the orphanage.

Oldana had left Ulan in 2002; the children 'graduate' at age 15 or 16. What a surprise then to be called down from my office a few weeks after my arrival to see her standing at the reception desk! She was still tiny and the lines on her face were that of a girl more than twice her age, but her beautiful smile lit up her face as I came down the steps. For a girl so frail, her hug was tight and strong. Her hands were calloused, but her face shone with joy. She had heard from the other children that I had moved to Taraz. She wanted me to come see her house, to meet her children and husband. It was hard to imagine this young girl with girls of her own.

The following week, my Kazakh colleagues, Assel and Aben, and I took off to find her house. When she had given directions they had seemed fairly simple. The day was bright and sunny and I expected the trip to be short and easy. However, I should have remembered to expect the unexpected.

Most Westerners can't begin to imagine the state of the roads in Kazakhstan. Though some major roads are improving, most of the back roads are full of potholes and driving them involves dodging livestock, donkey carts, pedestrians and other drivers, who act like they own the roads.

Oldana's directions had suggested only two turn-offs, but the actual trip had a lot more turns to it. We persevered though, and the road started to become more like a path between houses, seemingly placed at random. We stopped at intervals to ask bystanders for help. No one seemed to know of Oldana, but all said we were on the correct road.

The village was divided up into three areas, each with the same set of road names. The streets were unnervingly narrow, but Aben assured me the car would be able to squeeze through. As most of the inhabitants didn't have cars, I guess the road's width didn't matter much to them. The houses were *dachas*: small, mud brick homes with white painted plaster and sky blue metal roof and trim. They were originally built by city folk, to allow them to escape the summer heat and grow their own fruits and vegetables.

Spotting an elderly woman, we stopped to ask directions again. Victoria, a small woman with gray hair swirled up in a bun, had a welcoming smile. If she was surprised to have a rather lost American at her gate she didn't show it. Instead she graciously invited us in for tea. She showed us around her humble home and we shared the details of our quest. In response she jumped up and started clipping grapes that hung ripe from the arbor above and gathering tomatoes and cucumbers from the garden – to share with Oldana. She was sure that Oldana did not live on her street, but encouraged us to head to the next area of the village to a street of the same name. As we backed the car down the path (it was too narrow to turn around) she stood waving with a big smile on her face.

After a few more detours, we were told to go down the large hill on the left and turn right at the fifth road and we'd find her house. Once we had figured out what to count as roads, we found the narrow path that led to Oldana's house.

She and her husband, Daurin, who had also been raised in the orphanage, were trying to build a life for themselves. Despite the odds against them, they were working hard to succeed. They had scraped enough money together to buy this small *dacha*, measuring five by seven meters and in a state of disrepair. The plaster was crumbling off the walls and the patched metal roof revealed daylight when one looked up from the inside of the house. The small plot of land lay barren and muddy. An old metal barrier encircled a well with its beat-up rusty bucket attached to a rope. In the muddy field of a yard was only an outhouse, leaning precariously to one side.

As I looked at Oldana's tiny frame as she held her youngest, I was touched by the look of accomplishment on her face. There was hope in her eyes that the lives of her girls would be easier than her own life had been. Hope is not something you find often in orphaned children. Kazakhstan's statistics tell a bleak story, with less than 10 percent of orphaned children managing to build a life for themselves and many dying within the first five years of leaving the orphanage. Yet before me stood one young woman working hard to build a life for herself and her family.

Some Americans may have looked around and seen utter despair and poverty. What I saw was great promise and potential. Looking into the neighbor's yards I saw apricot and apple trees. I saw the remains of summer gardens, a good indication that the dirt was fertile. Even though the house obviously needed many repairs, it seemed to be structurally sound. My mind was whirling with the possibilities of what could be done here, although I was also mindful of not taking away their sense of accomplishment.

All their money had gone into purchasing the house, leaving no funds to repair the roof. Winter was coming and they had their two young girls, Eliana and Diana, to look after. After some discussion it was decided that if Daurin would provide labor then I would get supplies.

A couple of weeks later a work crew of six men, American and Kazakh, showed up to replace the roof. They removed and replaced the rotten timbers and installed a new metal roof. By nightfall the only task remaining was to finish off the gable ends and trim. I often wonder what the neighbors thought and, more importantly, what Eliana and Diana thought of having their home invaded, torn apart and then put back together. We brought a picnic lunch for us all to enjoy, and, typical of children, the girls enjoyed the chips and cookies as much as the *kolbasa* (sausage) and bread. The girls call me *apa,* which is Kazakh for aunt.

The following spring they put in a huge garden, including flowers to make the place look beautiful. During one visit I noticed an old donkey cart and got excited, thinking they had bought a donkey.

"No," was the answer. Daurin had found the old cart and was working on repairing it in the hopes of one day having a donkey. Seeing all the hard work they had done and the initiative they had shown, a friend and I talked over the idea of giving them a donkey as a gift. Friends of mine donated the funds and plans were made to meet Oldana and Daurin at the animal bazaar, a mostly male affair.

Daurin had never been to the animal bazaar, nor had he ever bought an animal. If he had grown up in a typical Kazakh home this would have been commonplace. It isn't unusual to see a small car driving down the road with a live animal (often a sheep) tied up in the backseat or in the trunk. The family will then slaughter the creature for a special celebration.

As we walked down the hill to where the donkeys were gathered, I could see the hesitation on Oldana and Daurin's faces. I wanted Daurin to take the lead in purchasing his donkey and fairly quickly he had pointed out a young colt. Next there was the matter of getting the donkey home. I have a friend in Kyrgyzstan who once delivered two donkeys to a family using the *marshrutka* (local minibus), but I was pretty sure that wouldn't go down well in Taraz. We had an SUV-like vehicle and I figured the donkey could sit in the back, but my co-worker didn't think that was a good idea. Daurin went off in search of a truck.

In Kazakhstan, bread is taken from the bakery to where it will be sold in small trucks. The truck beds are covered, and there is a small door at the back. This is exactly the kind of truck Daurin found in which to haul his donkey home. (I found myself imagining these trucks were used to haul animals on a Sunday and bread the rest of the week.) Oldana and Daurin bade goodbye after giving hugs and words of thanks. I couldn't wait to see what they would do with their new donkey.

I was astounded the next time I went to visit them. Daurin had used the donkey to haul dirt and straw and was manufacturing mud bricks. He had sold some to neighbors, but mostly he had used them to improve their home. I felt like a proud mama as they took me around their place and shared with great pride the results of their hard work. Oldana showed me how they had expanded their home by adding a small room. Daurin beamed as he opened the door to his new outbuilding to reveal the contents: coal, wood and canned vegetables from their garden. I didn't have words. Tears slid down my cheeks as I surveyed all that they had done.

That first journey to Kazakhstan in 2000 opened the door to a life I could never have imagined. With this came an opportunity to be part of something bigger than myself, to be humbled by the generosity and kindness of people half a world from where I started, and to find a place to call home.

In Search of the Third *Kebezhe*

by Francesco Le Rose

I opened my eyes at the ringing of my iPhone and mechanically grabbed it from the nightstand. I realized then it was the alarm clock. It was 6:50 am on a Saturday morning and my penultimate weekend in Atyrau, Kazakhstan. The room was filled with the sort of light that invites you to leap into action. I looked out of the window at the blue summer sky, the kind of blue that only Kazakhstan can offer, with not the slightest wisp of a cloud in sight. The 40° Celsius heat wiped from memory the –40° Celsius of the Kazakh winter.

I kept to my usual routine, but in a house now empty of voices. The absence of my wife and my children's laughter – sounds that usually kick started my day – was conspicuous. I remembered my wife's words before she and the kids had returned to Italy: "Remember, you have more than a month to find another *kebezhe*. I promised my mother. I don't want to disappoint her."

It was during her visit to Damba, a fishermen's village an hour's drive from Atyrau, that Monica had discovered the first *kebezhe*, a traditional piece of Kazakh furniture that is used in the yurt for storing food and tableware. A few days before her repatriation to Italy, she had left the comfort of our villa in the expat compound to spend the day in Damba with our two children, and to meet the parents of Sholpan, my children's first Kazakh nanny, who has since become a dear family friend. Sholpan, with her dark shining eyes, is the best friend an expat family could wish for. She speaks Kazakh, Russian and English, laughs and plays with the children, and is serious with the adults and always on hand to help.

Monica described this day as one of the most beautiful she had spent in Kazakhstan. I saw in her the traveler who loves to stray from the tourist routes to discover the essence of a place. She was so happy to have shared in the simplicity of a day with this family, enriched by their composed yet warm welcome. She was thrilled also to be in a place where ancient gestures and traditions capture your soul and to witness the nobility of this nomadic people. Today, she proudly tells others how our girls ate *beshbarmak* with their hands.

Monica had seen the *kebezhe* by chance, while paying a visit to an elderly relative of Sholpan. Resembling a small trunk with four legs, it was sixty centimeters high, one meter long and less than half a meter deep. There was a small door in the middle of the front, but in some more elaborate models there is a small drawer too. The feature that makes the *kebezhe* most attractive is the inlay on three of the four sides, with themes that symbolize Kazakh traditions painted in bright colors ranging from green to red to white, burgundy and yellow. Monica was immediately fascinated and whispered something to this effect in Sholpan's ear.

"Really?" said Sholpan. "Do you like it?"

"Oh, yes, it's beautiful," my wife replied. "I'd love to take one home as a souvenir."

"We might be able to buy this one," said Sholpan, "but it's better that you stay out of the deal for the time being. Let me ask my mother the best way to go about it."

Accompanied by her mother, Sholpan returned a few hours later to the old relative, who accepted the offer to buy the *kebezhe* for a few thousand tenge.

The day after the visit to Damba, while proudly showing it to Ainur, our nanny at the time, Monica discovered that *her* grandmother also owned a *kebezhe*. Two days later the two *kebezhe* were standing together, side by side in our house. They looked similar only in shape; the inlays and colors chosen by the respective craftsmen made each a unique piece.

I was on my second sip of coffee, which is made always with my Bialetti coffee machine (my faithful friend in my expatriate adventures), when I saw the minibus had arrived, on time as usual.

My mission today was to fulfill my wife's wish for a third *kebezhe*. With a driver organized by my company and Sholpan as interpreter, I was heading to the mythical village of Sarayshyk; about a two-hour drive from Atyrau and once a leg of the ancient silk route. Little of its splendor remains today, although recent archaeological excavations have brought to light some important findings, such as houses of the ancient city's first inhabitants and a variety of crockery. A few dozen families live here and there is one museum to share the village's antiquities. We believed we might find a *kebezhe* in one of the old houses in Sarayshyk.

Sholpan revealed our destination to the driver, whose reply was a look of bewilderment. After only a few minutes we left behind the traffic and city houses. This was the first time I had left the city without my wife and girls. I became aware of this because there it felt unfamiliar to have no distractions, no shouting, laughter or nappies. My eyes lost themselves in the boundless expanse of the steppe, split in half by a long, straight and endless road. I felt like a sailor in the middle of the sea, for the bushes and grasses rippled like waves. On the horizon, perhaps to make the Ural River's journey less monotonous, were an infinite expanse of bush, dotted with yellow and red flowers, and the odd sand dune. I could not but think of the days when camels and horses were the undisputed lords of this land, together with their nomadic masters.

Suddenly, a sign appeared out of nowhere; I could make out 'Sarayshyk' in the Cyrillic script. There was a kind of sculpture nearby, but the minibus was going too fast for me to understand what it represented. We reached a junction, where a sign on the right read 'Museum'. The driver stopped and turned to us for guidance. On the opposite side of the road I could see a man and a woman coming towards us, walking arm in arm.

"Please Sholpan," I said, "ask them where we might find some antique furniture."

I looked out the window, listening to the conversation in Kazakh. The woman was smiling, covering her mouth, and Sholpan too was amused. The man gestured in the direction opposite to that of the museum.

"He suggests we try to look in the oldest part of the village," said Sholpan. "It is located in the area around the archeological excavations."

The wind had picked up and the dust rose all around us. The official road seemed to disappear and the minibus started zigzagging to avoid large shallow potholes. We stopped in front of a gate manned by a guard in a sort of wooden hut. I realised we had reached the excavation area. The guard became excited on hearing of our interest in antiques and invited us to come inside.

"He doesn't know where we can find a *kebezhe*," explained Sholpan, "but would be happy to let us take a tour of the excavation area."

I replied that we didn't have much time, as I wanted to make it back to Atyrau by lunch. Thanking the guard, we boarded the minibus again, unsure of where to head next. I looked around me at the large open space out of which arose a series of old houses. The houses were small and square, white and sand in colour, with wooden doors and window frames painted blue.

Sand was circling in the air, denying me a clear view. Suddenly, however, I noticed two old ladies, probably neighbors, chatting in front of a blue door. Their clothes were white and each had a scarf around her face for protection from the wind. Sholpan was a little reluctant to approach them, but finally agreed to make one last attempt. After Sholpan had explained the reason for our visit, one of the women pointed to a house about a hundred meters away with wooden fences about two meters high. On reaching the house, Sholpan knocked at the blue door. A dog started barking and after a few seconds a small door within a gate to the right of the house opened. Sholpan exchanged a few words with the old man, who peeped out. Then she turned to me, smiling, and told me to step inside as the man opened the gate.

I could not believe my eyes. Within this large fence was a world in itself: piles of junk, and mostly rusty iron, were the backdrop to a series of small stables and three yurts. I could distinguish bicycle frames, automotive parts, trucks, sheets of metal, and containers of various shapes as well as a host of parts from who knows what else.

The man now entered the house via the porch, which was covered with a creeper to create shade. After a few seconds, he came out, accompanied by a sturdy, wrinkled woman in a pair of blue pants and a black blouse. She greeted us and smiled.

Sholpan revealed our goal. The women looked in the direction of the yurts, before heading for one with a blue engraved door and beckoning us to follow her. She opened the wooden door and bent down to enter. Once in the yurt we were surrounded by a series of shelves containing boxes, crates, carpets, bottles, and a range of furniture. And there, on the middle shelf to my right, covered with a thin layer of dust, was a *kebezhe*! It was burgundy in color with inlays that perfectly camouflaged the little cupboard door, only the small doorknob giving it away. I could hardly contain my joy at having found it. Helped by her husband, the woman brought it out into the daylight. She also produced a carpet and recreated a scene of how the piece of furniture would once have lain in a yurt.

"It's perfect!" I whispered to Sholpan. "Let's get going with the bargaining… and try to include the carpet too!"

The requested price was way below my estimation of the items' value: for less than one hundred euros I bought both. A few minutes later we were back on the minibus with the third *kebezhe*. While my eyes again took in the view of the steppe, I phoned my wife.

"*Ciao cara.*"

"Hi, where are you?" she replied. "I tried to call you at home."

"I'm in the steppe."

"In the steppe? Doing what?"

"Do you remember your wish for a third *kebezhe*?"

"Yes, of course!"

"Well, mission accomplished!"

The Long Horse Ride: Journey Across the Steppe

by Rowena Haigh & Yolanda Cook

The Long Horse Ride is an endurance ride that started shortly after the 2008 Beijing Olympics, crossing China, Central Asia and Europe, before entering London in time for the 2012 London Olympics. The horse ride aimed to raise funds for charities within the countries it crossed. It entered Kazakhstan in June 2010 at Korgas and headed west towards Kyzylorda, before heading north towards Atyrau and then crossing into Russia at Astrakhan. Two expats in Kazakhstan at the time joined organizer and lead rider Megan Lewis on different legs of her journey.

Rowena Haigh took part in various legs of the ride, including the first trial and the final leg in the UK. Here she gives us a glimpse into her month-long journey across the Kazakh Steppe, which began in late March 2011, at the start of spring. Rowena covered about 2,500 kilometres, excluding the final week's ride into London.

I had found a lovely six-year-old stallion in Atyrau, who I christened Bolashak after the company that helped sponsor me. My next challenge was to transport him to our designated starting point in Kyzylorda, where Megan had placed her horse, Zorbee, over the winter. I had driven the Atyrau-Kyzylorda road in the autumn and knew how terrible it was, particularly the stretch from Atyrau to Aktobe. There seemed to be more craters than road and some were bigger than our little Niva car! I was concerned about how Bolashak would cope with being bumped about in the back of a truck for three days, especially as time was of the essence, and he would have to be ready to start the ride as soon as we got there. While poring over a map, I noticed a railway line directly from Atyrau to Kyzylorda!

As I began to follow an endless paper trail that led to and from various small offices staffed by bemused employees of the Kazakh railway establishment, it became apparent that no one, let alone a single foreign woman, had ever tried to transport a horse to Kyzylorda this way. Maybe to put me off, I was told I had to travel with the horse in the wagon. When the railway authorities realised I was serious, they became increasingly worried about my comfort, telling me that the wagon would be unbearably cold and insisting that I arrange some type of camp bed for the nights. Overall though, the authorities were incredibly helpful if rather incredulous about the whole adventure. They promised to try and ensure that my wagon was not left in sidings for longer than necessary and that I would be sent south as quickly as possible; and so it was that I found myself one morning at a yard behind the main passenger station loading Bolly and supplies for the next three days.

My camp bed and a chair were placed with great ceremony in the middle of the wagon, so I could look out of the sliding door as I travelled across the steppe. There were containers of water for both of us and more than enough warm clothing and bedding (or so I thought). With due ceremony, and several photos with various officials, I set off. My progress was to be reported to my husband as I travelled along the line.

The journey was a wonderful, unusual experience. There were looks of amazement on the faces of passing train drivers when they saw me looking out of my cattle wagon and endless conversations with surprised policemen checking the trains for stowaways – not to mention lots of admiration for the ever-patient Bolashak. The first night was unbelievably cold. I had to sleep in all my clothes and even considered putting up my tent so I could have some more insulation. The wagon remained cold over the next few days, but it was a little better when I eventually managed to close the vents that had been opened to give me some light. (Light was an issue as the wagon had metal sides.) Unfortunately, the only door I could open was on the opposite side to the sun all the way and so I didn't have the chance to let the wagon warm up with sunshine. Aside from the physical discomfort, there was also the problem of never knowing where I was when we stopped in a siding or how long we would pause. Sometimes the stop was a matter of minutes and other times it went on for hours, and I was always nervous of straying too far from the wagon in case it started moving again. Fortunately, we made such good progress that we arrived before Megan, who had left on the Almaty Express a few days after us.

Back in the saddle
On meeting up, Megan, John Smallwood – a photographer who was to join us on his bicycle for two weeks to document the ride – and I headed out to Zorbee's temporary winter residence. After a day of preparing the horses and being served a lavish lunch by our hosts, we set off with an hour or so of daylight left; just enough for us to feel that we were back on the road again.

The first couple of days are always tough on a ride like this as it takes time to get used to the long days in the saddle and sleeping on a bedroll in a tent. However, when sitting around the campfire with a vodka or two to warm you, watching the sun set over the steppe and listening to the chomping of the horses, it is all worth it.

Heading north, we rode along the route of the Syr Darya, catching glimpses of the elusive river through the trees and reeds. It is difficult to describe the excitement of seeing and crossing the famous rivers of the Asian-European landmass. Their names are magical and exotic, faraway entities that have been marked on a map, and then suddenly you are upon them, and instantly you know what this part of the world looks like.

The joys of the steppe

The gift of riding a horse across the face of the world is *time*; you can't rush through anything. There was time to think, to contemplate what it might be like to call this home. The downside was that on some days the steppe felt endless, and then we had to rely on mental strength to keep positive and interested. We found that looking out for life on the ground gave us things to think about! We looked for footprints in the sand – the strangest were left by a tortoise. (We were unsure what the prints were until half an hour later, when we found a tortoise on our route.) We were particularly eager to find native Kazakh tulips and, after five days of searching, we saw our first yellow tulip growing up out of the sandy ground. We spent at least half an hour photographing it. Later on, when the tulips became more frequent, we still could not resist calling out in excitement.

As we rode further north, spring followed us. The weather was kind, neither too hot nor too cold, and there was green grass for the horses to graze on. We also found glorious clumps of irises and many other flowers we did not know the names of. At night we lay in our tents listening to the wolves howling. At one campsite, the locals were so concerned about our horses being found by wolves that they put the horses in a coral for safety. We were a little put out that we were not put in there too and we had an oft disturbed night listening to the howls that seemed to surround our tents and come closer and closer. We found we had to be careful about scorpions too. The first couple of nights, Megan had left her boots out at night, but she soon stopped doing this after I found five scorpions under my tent one morning.

Things to celebrate
We camped above the city of Baikonur on the eve of Uri Gagarin's first flight from there exactly 50 years earlier. We decided to hold our own ceremony on the day of the anniversary. At exactly 9 am we stood on the brow of a hill overlooking the cosmodrome, where we raised a glass of Heaven vodka to Uri. We thought it an appropriate brand of vodka for the occasion.

As we later passed the city, we noticed lots of joggers and cyclists about and assumed they were celebrating the event with a triathlon. However, we discovered there was an even more impressive feat on the go when, a few hours later, we came across a bus that looked as if it had broken down. We were a little nervous as there appeared to be lots of people in their underwear roaming around on the road. Megan approached ahead of me and, as she advanced, they all rushed over, photographing her and waving for me to come and join them. We learned that they had chosen to honour Uri Gagarin with a super marathon! They were running in relay teams (some in baggy underwear, others in running shorts) from Baikonur to Moscow, 2,500 kilometres away, and estimated it would take them three months. Some of the runners were former Olympians from the Paralympic Games. It was inspiring to meet this group along our own challenging journey.

The kindness of strangers

There were always small moments that helped to lift our spirits, usually inspired by people's kindness and curiosity. A gallant gentleman pursued us on his grey horse, to check we were okay, and to make sure we had food. When we assured him that we had supplies, he disappeared, muttering, and we presumed he had turned back, thinking we were lunatics. In fact he had gone home to fetch us some fresh camel milk to fortify ourselves.

We also had regular visits from the security guards on the pipeline track. They would come and check on our progress, often calling in at our campsite at night to make sure all was in order. They were cheerful and friendly fellows who always brought us a laugh.

Rest and illness

After two weeks, we reached Aralsk, where John left us and Megan and I relaxed in the relative luxury of the Aral Hotel for a couple of nights. The beds were comfortable and we eventually managed to get enough hot water to dribble over ourselves for our first decent wash in over two weeks. I am sure that the population of Aralsk was even more grateful than we were! As these were rest days, we took the opportunity to be tourists and spent a fascinating day seeing the reclaimed Aral Sea and the ship graveyard.

Leaving Aralsk, we found ourselves riding along tracks and small roads linking settlements and oil pipeline stations while following the railway line that I had been on weeks earlier. Gradually the tracks left the steppe behind and we came to sand dunes. We had been concerned about getting our little truck through this terrain as it was not a four-wheel drive, but Barzhan, our driver, did a fantastic job nursing it along tracks it was definitely not designed to take on! Our worries had been misdirected, for it was Bolly who was to delay us. He became ill and began to struggle with the daily journey. We could not see what had caused his sudden decline, just that he was losing weight and had very little energy. As leaving him behind was not an option, I had a long walk ahead of me, leading (or dragging) a rather grumpy and slightly depressed horse to our final destination at Shalkar. Normally a fairly easygoing horse, Bolly became annoyed with me constantly urging him on and he eventually turned on me, giving me a good bite on my chest and drawing blood. By now we were both feeling quite sorry for ourselves and we must have been a sight to behold as we ploughed onwards. We slogged on over 90 kilometres of sand dunes, a huge challenge for both of us. We were very relieved to make it to Shalkar, where Bolly could have a rest (and finally recuperate) until Barzhan came to collect him a week later, while I headed home.

Looking back

Once again I found myself on the train, this time heading home to Atyrau. Gazing out onto the steppe as it sped by, I longed to be back out there, slowly crossing it, watching the skies, feeling the breeze, listening to birds and looking out for elusive wildlife. There is something magical about the endless steppe.

It has a subtle beauty, one you need to slow down to appreciate. The small nuances of light and shade, the diversity of plant life due to changes in the landscape, the small low-growing flowers, the soaring birds in endless blue skies… these are memories that will live with me forever.

Yolanda Cook, also on Bolashak, joined Megan for two weeks in May 2012, travelling from Embi to Baygonin and covering about 360 kilometres.

Relocating to Kazakhstan came with many challenges: a foreign language, a different culture and unfamiliar foods. Along with these various tribulations came the vast open steppe, wild tulips, camels, friendly, hospitable people and many, many horses. It is on the steppe that I found a passion for the Kazakh people, their habits and their love of horses; it is here that I left a small part of my heart.

It is said that most nomadic Kazakhs learned to ride before they can walk! The horse has always been essential to Kazakh culture: it played an important role in exploring the steppe and moving the yurts and possessions from place to place. Even today horses are a basic element of Kazakh nutrition, with both their milk and meat being consumed. Ever since I can remember I have wanted to live on the vast open steppe with my horse, experience life as a nomad and get to know this culture. Never did I think that I would get the chance to do it…

Out on the steppe

The weather here can easily jump from −40° Celsius in winter to 40° Celsius in summer. I was lucky to be out on the steppe in May, with its milder temperatures, and to experience enormous open spaces filled with green grasses and several small, landlocked lakes. No traffic (for it's a terrain too rugged for vehicles), no man-made noise... just peace and tranquility, the odd birdsong, caravans of camels and herds of horses. We carried water for the horses in drums on the back-up truck. Of course it was rationed, because we never knew when we would reach the next watering hole. Every night before bedtime I would take a small amount of water, head off to my tent, have a wash down, add a sprinkling of baby powder, and I was fresh as a daisy the following morning.

There are no phone lines or electricity cables either, just the friendly smiles from the herders on the steppe as they extended invites to join them for a cup of tea. They would surprise us on horseback, approaching with thundering hooves across grass-laden hills, appearing out of nowhere. I can imagine the two of us must have stuck out like a sore thumb: two Western women riding out on the steppe with our horses and completely different tack! They would flash a friendly smile and indicate to their house over the next couple of hills, where a warm cup of tea awaited. When our horses needed their thirst quenched or a rest, the herders would jump at the opportunity to take the animals into safety and tend to all their needs.

I soon learned that when you go into a Kazakh house for a cup of tea, you do not get to leave after one cup! Tea is a whole affair and never just 'a quick cuppa'. The tea is poured from a *samovar* to which they add a few scoops of milk with a wooden spoon. It is served in a special Asian-style cup (called a *piala* or *kese*), or in a small wooden bowl and accompanied by several nibbly bits. Apparently, if you are served a half-bowl your company is still welcome. When you are served a full cup, it is time to get moving. I can happily say that we had numerous half-cups!

Sometimes a herder would join us for a short ride on his horse. Then, all of a sudden and without warning, he would gallop off into the distance, probably to go and tend to his daily chores. Small houses dotted the steppe every few kilometres and I was amazed that inhabitants could make a living in the middle of nowhere, with no shops within a few days' journey. It dawned on me that this is how they have been doing it for centuries.

During the ride we often came to a *gastenitsa* (small café or restaurant) that would serve us a delicious, hearty meal. I learned to sample and love many traditional dishes: *manti* (an Uighur dish looks like steamed bun filled with meat, onion and pumpkin), *laghman* (an Uighur meat soup with homemade noodles) and *baursak* (traditional Kazakh bread), to name but a few of my favourites.

Storm on the steppe

A few days into our journey, dark rain clouds were threatening to cut our day short. The driver had gone up ahead to find our camp for the night, but failed to meet us at the roadside as he did every night. By pure chance, we spotted him out in the distance and rode up to him, only to find that the truck was stuck in the mud.

That difficulty aside, he had managed to find an idyllic spot: a clear lake, horses lining the horizon, and a tree. After feeding, rugging and tethering the horses, pitching our tents, pouring our sundowners and starting to cook our supper, we managed to get the truck out of the mud. By this time the storm clouds had decided to dump rain on us. It was thundering and we prayed that our tree would not get struck by lightning. We finished our dinner in the truck, our only shelter. Despite the omnipresent leaks in the tarpaulin that covered the back, we remained relatively dry.

When we decided to call it a night and head for our sleeping quarters, the wind was still howling, with thunder and lightning at full force. Our tents were almost blown flat by the force of the wind. I took off my boots and stepped into my tent, only to find everything, even my bed, drifting in water up to my ankles. My tent clearly was *not* waterproof!

Everyone was already off to dreamland and I was out in the pouring rain. The only solution was to grab my damp sleeping bag and head for the equally damp truck. I got in the back, cleared a patch between the food, hay, barrels of water and our supplies, tried to plug a few dripping holes with plastic and nodded off to sleep. It was a cold and wet sleep, but I made it through the night and woke wetter and stronger, though with an aching body!

The nomadic experience
Having been able to experience the arid land of Kazakhstan on the back of a horse, in a country where horses have always been the core of the culture, was a special adventure for me, a fellow horse-lover. In Atyrau it is very easy to look past each other and get on with our lives. Being out on the steppe, experiencing what it is like to be a nomad, you get to see people for who they really are. No flashy cars or big houses. Instead you find a yurt fit for a king, a meal prepared with all the host family has to offer, tea accompanied by a hearty smile… an invitation with no ulterior motives. I found real people with a passion for their culture, a culture so rich and so different from the Western life I know.

Note: Megan, Rowena and Chinese rider Peng Wenchao arrived in Greenwich, London, on 22 July 2012, five days before the official opening ceremony of the Olympics. See www.thelonghorseride. com for more details on the route and its riders.

Resources

Books

Aifeld, V.F. (2006) *The Land of Enchanted Horizons.* Almaty: Publisher

Aitken, J. (2012) *Kazakhstan: Surprises and Stereotypes After 20 Years of Independence.* London-New York: Continuum International Publishing

Aitken, J. (2009) *Nazarbayev and the Making of Kazakhstan: From Communism to Capitalism.* London-New York: Continuum International Publishing

Aitmatov, C. (1988) *The Day Lasts More Than a Hundred Years.* Bloomington: Indiana University Press

Brummell P. (2008) *Kazakhstan.* Buckinghamshire: Bradt Travel Guides

Canetta, E. (2006) *L'inguaribile Tristezza del Saggio: Una Ricerca sulla Cultura Kazaka* [Italian]. Genoa: Marietti Editore

Dave, B., (2007) *Kazakhstan: Ethnicity, Language and Power.* New York: Routledge

Facchini, F. (2008) *Popoli della Yurta. Il Kazakhstan tra Le Origini e La Modernità* [Italian]. Rimini: Jaca Book

Fergus M. & Jandosova J. (2003) *Kazakhstan: Coming of Age.* London: Stacey International

Ivashenko, A.A. (2008) *Reserves and National Parks of Kazakhstan.* Almaty: Almatykitap

Kenzheakhmetly, S. (2007) *Kazakh Traditions and Customs.* Almaty: Almatykitap

Kuandykov, B. (2008) *Keys to the Caspian Shelf.* London: Meridian Petroleum

Lamb, S. (2009) *Sixteen Months of Mutton: Meat-eating Journeys through Kazakhstan, Kyrgyztan, and Mongolia.* Charleston: Booksurge Publishing

Laroni-Marsilio, N. (Ed.) (2009) *Il Profumo dell'Erba* [Italian]. Venice: Marsilio Editori

Laumulin, C. & Laumulin, M. (2009) *The Kazakhs: Children of the Steppes.* Leiden: Global Oriental

Ligabue, G. & Arbore-Popescu, G. (2000) *I Cavalieri delle Steppe: Memoria delle Terre del Kazakhstan* [Italian]. Milan: Electa Editore

Mamraimov, A. (2009) *Sacred Places on the Great Silk Road.* Almaty: Almatykitap

Mayhew, B., Bloom, G., & Clammer, P. (2010) *Central Asia.* London: Lonely Planet

Mesh, S. & Mesh, S. (2003) *You've Got Mail from Kazakhstan.* Higganum: Higganum Hill Books

Nazarbayev, N. & Thatcher, M. (foreword) (2008) *The Kazakhstan Way.* London: Stacey International Publishers

Olcott, M.B. (2002) *Kazakhstan: Unfulfilled Promise.* Washington: Carnegie Endowment for International Peace

Olcott, M.B. (1995) *The Kazakhs.* San Franscisco: Hoover Institution Press

Pomme Clayton, S. (2005) *Tales Told in Tents: Stories from Central Asia.* London: Frances Lincoln Children's Books

Robbins, C. (2008) *In Search of Kazakhstan: The Land That Disappeared.* London: Profile Books

Romanov, I. & Zhandauletov, V. (2010) *Kazakhstan.* Almaty: Almatykitap

Schreiber, D. (2008) *Kazakhstan: Nomadic Routes from Caspian to Altai.* Hong Kong: Airphoto International Ltd.

Shayakhmetov, M. (2006) *The Silent Steppe: The Story of a Kazakh Nomad Under Stalin*. New York City: Overlook Press

Shayakhmetov, M. (2013) *A Kazakh Teacher's Story: Surviving the Silent Steppe*. London: Stacey International Publishers

Winner, T.G. (1980) *The Oral Art and Literature of the Kazakhs of Russian Central Asia (Folklore of the World)*. North Stratford: Ayer Co Pub

Yakushkin, V. & Yakushkin, I. (2002) *Kazakhstan*. Almaty: Berei

Films

Abdrashev, R. (Director) (2008) *The Gift to Stalin [Podarok Stalinu]*. Almaty: Kazakhfilm Studios et al

Amirkulov, A. (Director) (1991) *The Fall of Otrar [Gibel Otrara]*. Almaty: Kazakhfilm Studios et al

Baigazin, E. (Director) (2013) *Harmony Lessons [Uroki Garmonii]*. Almaty: Kazakhfilm Studios et al

Bodrov, S. & Passer, I. (Directors) (2005) *Nomad: The Warrior [Köshpendiler]*. Almaty: Kazakhfilm Studios et al

Dvortsevoy, S. (Director) (2008) *Tulpan*. Almaty: Eurasia Film

Satayev, A. (Director) (2011) *Myn Bala*. Almaty: Kazakhfilm Studios et al

Websites, blogs and online videos

Arts & culture

http://www.abay.nabrk.kz/index.php?lang=en

http://www.heritagenet.unesco.kz

http://www.kazakhdervish.com
http://www.ocamagazine.com

Community work & NGOs
http://eng.alemproject.kz
http://www.j127ranch.org
http://www.larca.org/

Expats in Kazakhstan
http://aktauexpats.wordpress.com
http://atyrauexpats.tripod.com
http://ersatzexpat.blogspot.it
http://expat.nursat.kz/
http://kazakhnomad.wordpress.com
http://machinkaz.blogsnel.nl
http://www.expat-blog.com/en/destination/asia/kazakhstan
http://www.expatclic.com (limited content)
http://www.expatexchange.com/kazakhstan/liveinkazakhstan.html
http://www.expatwomen.com/expat-women-countries/expat-women-living-in-kazakhstan.php
http://www.internations.org/almaty-expats
http://www.internations.org/astana-expats

General information
http://aboutkazakhstan.com
http://visitkazakhstan.kz/en
http://welcometokazakhstan.com
http://wikitravel.org/en/Kazakhstan
http://www.astana.kz/en
http://www.discovery-kazakhstan.com
http://www.kazakhstan.orexca.com

http://www.lonelyplanet.com/kazakhstan
http://www.worldtravelguide.net/kazakhstan

News & media
http://azh.kz/en
http://www.edgekz.com

YouTube videos
Aiman Mussakhajayeva (famous Kazakh violinist)
Qara Jorga (traditional Kazakh dance)

Glossary of Terms

A

akim: mayor (Kazakh/Russian)

amin: Muslim gesture of thanks that involves cupping the hands and passing them down the face

apa: aunt (Kazakh)

aul: village (Kazakh)

azhe: grandmother (Kazakh)

B

banya: steam bath (Russian)

baursak: traditional Kazakh bread (Kazakh)

beshbarmak: traditional Kazakh dish of horse, beef, camel and lamb's meat, served with dough and sprinkled with onions (Kazakh)

besik: baby cradle (Kazakh)

borsh: soup with meat and noodles (Kazakh/Russian)

blynys: thin pancakes folded into triangles, served with sour cream or honey (Russian)

C

chagala: seagull (Kazakh)

chai: tea (Kazakh/Russian)

D

dacha: countryside or small countryside house (Russian)

dah: yes (Russian)

devushka: lady (Russian)

dom: house (Russian)

dvor: courtyard (Russian)

E

F

G

gastenitsa: small café or restaurant (Kazakh)

Golandia: Holland (Kazakh/Russian)

H

horosho: good (Russian)

I

Ia ne ponimayu: I don't understand (Russian)

J

K

kazan: cauldron-style cooking pot (Kazakh)

kebezhe: traditional Kazakh piece of furniture that is used in the yurt for storing food and tableware (Kazakh)

kese: Asian-style tea cup or small bowl (Kazakh)

kespe: homemade noodles (Kazakh)

klassi: hopscotch (children's game) (Russian)

kobyz: ancient Kazakh instrument with two strings (Kazakh)

kolbasa: sausage (Russian)

kurdas: men or women who are born in the same year (Kazakh)

kymiz: horse milk (Kazakh)

L

laghman: Uighur meat soup with homemade noodles (Kazakh/Russian)

M

manti: Uighur dish resembling a steamed bun filled with meat, onion and pumpkin (Kazakh/Russian)

marshrutka: local minibus (Russian)

menia zavut: my name is (Russian)

menin atym: my name is (Kazakh)

N

normalno: normal, fine or okay (Russian)

nyet: no (Russian)

O

Ochen pryatno: Nice to meet you (Russian)

P

palau: Uzbek dish of layered rice, often served with flat bread (Uzbek)

peevah: beer (Russian)

pervy sneg: first snow (Russian)

piala: Asian-style tea cup or brand of tea (Kazakh/Russian)

pirozhky: fresh potato pies (Russian)

plov: Russian dish: meat with rice and carrots; similar to Uzbek palau (Russian)

privet: hi (Russian)

pryatki: hide-and-seek (Russian)

Q

R

rahmet: thank you (Kazakh)

S

samovar: traditional water boiler that looks like a kettle with a tap (Russian)

semechki: roasted sunflower seeds (Russian)
shashlyk: skewered meat (Russian)
shorpo: broth made from mutton (Kazakh)
Shto..?: What is..? (Russian)
shubat: camel's milk (Kazakh)
sneg: snow (Russian)
sobaka: dog (Russian)
sukhariki: dried bread cubes with different flavors (Russian)
svetafor: traffic lights (Russian)

T

U

V

veniki: birch leaves (Russian)
Vsyo normalno devushka, seichas ne holodno: Everything's okay lady, it's not cold anymore (Russian)

W

X

Y

Z

zdrastvuite: hello (Russian)

About Monica Neboli

Monica Neboli (Lecco, Italy, 1969) has always been fascinated by other cultures. Before getting married, she backpacked all over the world. She then lived abroad with her husband and two daughters from 2006 until 2011, when she returned to her home country. During those five years abroad, she lived in Egypt and Kazakhstan, working as a coach to expat families, assisting them in adjusting harmoniously to their host country. While in Egypt, she wrote a booklet, '*Benvenuti al Cairo*' ['Welcome to Cairo'], for expat families arriving in Cairo, in collaboration with GIE (*Gruppo Italiani in Egitto*: a group for Italians in Egypt) and the Italian Embassy. While in Kazakhstan, she ran a seminar called: 'Fundamentals of living in Kazakhstan' to enable the expat community to learn more about the culture and history of their host country. Monica and her family enjoyed experiencing the many different cultures and peoples of Kazakhstan, and it was this that inspired her to compile a book of expat experiences in Kazakhstan. She has two daughters, Eleonora (6) and Agata (4), who are happily growing up as citizens of the world. Monica currently works in the corporate university of an oil company in Italy.

Monica Neboli
www.kzexpatstories.com
neboli@alice.it

About the Authors

Gualtiero Bestetti

Gualtiero Bestetti (Monza, Italy, 1977) is a nuclear engineer who has been working for seven years in the oil and gas industry. He first worked in Italy, then London, and in 2011 he and his wife relocated with their one-year-old son to Atyrau, Kazakhstan. Central Asia gave him a second son and a new perspective on life. He considers their time in Kazakhstan as one of the most interesting and exciting experiences of his life. He met people from all over the world and learned how to enjoy life with few and simple things. He currently lives in Italy, and is awaiting the next adventure.

Roberto Boltri

Roberto Boltri (Ampezzo, Italy, 1946) graduated with a degree in Environmental Sciences before working as an environmental engineer from 1972 to 1996 for a leading multinational corporation, working mainly in environmental and water resources management projects in Africa (Somalia, Algeria and Libya) and Asia (Uzbekistan). He then led international volunteer projects for international NGOs, the United Nations (UN) and the European Union (EU), in Bosnia and Herzegovina, Kazakhstan, Tajikistan, Uzbekistan and Kyrgyzstan. He has repeatedly been an international observer of elections for the Organisation for Economic Cooperation and Development (OECD). In 2006, he published the book *Un Esubero in Turkestan* [*Retired in Turkestan*]. Roberto is retired and lives in Kazakhstan.

Nina Buonaiuto

Nina Buonaiuto (Santa Fe, New Mexico, USA, 1977) is a teacher at QSI, the American international school in Astana. She has lived there with her husband and daughter for two years, but has "an embarrassing lack of Russian". "I like to think I'm too busy," she says, "but really I just haven't tried hard enough." Before Astana, she lived in China (where she did try to learn Chinese). She plans to move back to the United States someday and have simple camping vacations, recycle her plastics, have a garden, and shop at a local farmers' market that sells free-range eggs. "This is what I dream of when I'm stuck in big city traffic," she says.

Victoria Charbonneau

Victoria Charbonneau (Richmond, Virginia, USA, 1961) describes herself as a "Jack of all trades, master of none", because her life experiences have been so diverse. For example, she has worked on a dairy farm, as well as for a livestock dealer. She has also worked in construction, taught in the ESL department at Virginia Commonwealth University, worked with youth and the homeless in the US, been involved in foster care and hosted exchange students, *and* she has a general understanding of veterinary medicine. She is also a gifted artist and has an uncanny knack for working with children. She believes God gave her a huge heart for those overlooked and forgotten by society. She started going to Kazakhstan every year from 2000 until she moved there full-time in 2009. Learn more about Victoria's work with orphans and widows in distress in Kazakhstan at J127 Ranch/Artists for Community Transformation International on her website and blog: www.j127ranch.org.

Yolanda Cook

Yolanda Cook (Cape Town, South Africa, 1969) has had a curious mind since she was little and it didn't take long for her to decide that she wanted to travel. As a young woman, she lived and worked abroad for five years, au pairing in Italy and Greece; as a result she learnt to speak Greek fluently. Now, many years later, she is happily married and a mother of two children, aged 11 and 12. Yolanda is an avid animal lover, and is particularly passionate about horses. She enjoys the arts, writing and reading, and is always open to the next adventure. She is continuing her studies on various animal subjects to keep her curious nature satisfied. She and her husband enjoy the outdoors when they are home in Africa on holidays. After three years in Singapore, the family lives in Atyrau, Kazakhstan, with the goal of enjoying what life has to offer.

Stanley Currier

Stanley Currier (Los Angeles, California, USA, 1975) works for KIMEP University in Almaty, Kazakhstan. He started his career in education as an assistant language teacher on the Japan Exchange and Teaching Programme (JET) in Japan, and subsequently as a Peace Corps Volunteer in Kazakhstan. He then spent five years in the non-profit sector in Almaty, travelling extensively throughout Kazakhstan, Kyrgyzstan, Tajikistan and Uzbekistan promoting education exchange opportunities for Central Asian youth. Stanley has also served as a political affairs officer in the UN Tajikistan Office of Peace-building. He has spent over 10 years in Central Asia, and finds 'home' in both California and Kazakhstan.

Jacyntha England

Jacyntha England (Vancouver, Canada, 1967) has been active in international education for the past 20 years. She taught English in Almaty, Kazakhstan from 2004 to 2008. During her time there, she fell in love with the warmth and spontaneity of the cultures and communities who call Kazakhstan their home, and enjoyed many moments in the cafés, theatres and mountains of the city known as the 'father of apples'. She left Kazakhstan in 2008 for a job in hot and humid Singapore, where she misses the winters of Central Asia and the cries of "first snow" in its streets and schoolyards. Jacyntha has an MFA in Creative Writing from Canada's Simon Fraser University and has published numerous short stories, poems and articles in magazines, journals and anthologies. She sees writing as a way of expressing herself as she explores different countries and cultures, and is active in many writing groups and forums.

Kristina M. Gray

Kristina M. Gray (Crookston, Minnesota, USA, 1955) first arrived at Almaty's airport on 1 May 1993 as a Peace Corps trainer to the first volunteers destined to be English teachers across Kazakhstan. For her, it was *not* love at first sight, particularly given those first four scorching summer months in Almaty. However, she did end up marrying the American she met the day after her arrival in the country. The pair continued their relationship while she was a Fulbright scholar in Bishkek, Kyrgyzstan, just over the Tian Shan mountains, for the next few years. Thereafter they worked and taught in the Washington, D.C. area and spent seven years teaching in Kiev, Ukraine. The couple then returned to Kazakhstan in the fall of 2007, and Kristina taught at KIMEP University, at the same location where she had trained 30 PCVs (Peace Corps Volunteers). In those 14 years since she first arrived in Almaty, the city had changed significantly and Kristina found that life for expats had improved. Her final year in the country was spent in Nazarbayev University in Astana, where she started a professional development programme for 10 Kazakh teachers from Orken Intellectual Schools. She hopes to return to visit her former students and friends; until then, Facebook and Skype help with keeping in touch. Find Kristina's blog at http://kazakhnomad.wordpress.com.

Rowena Haigh

Rowena Haigh (Hong Kong, 1965) has long had family connections in the Far East. As a child, she learnt to ride Borneo pony stallions at the Hong Kong Jockey Club. After attending Warwick University in England, she went into teaching, initially in the UK, but later in the Middle East, where she met her husband Matt. Rowena has lived and travelled abroad extensively, including a solo trip to China in 1996, and a honeymoon through the 'Stans' and China in 2001. From 2005 to 2007, she and Matt spent two years living in the Northwest Frontier Province of Pakistan. During their time there, they not only attended the famous Shandur polo tournament in the Hindu Kush, but also trekked on foot to Baroghil on the Afghan border to be among the few people to experience the highest polo tournament in the world, featuring both horses and yaks! Rowena joined The Long Horse Ride whenever possible, allowing for the restrictions of a young family. She took part in the first trial leg – crossing the Gobi desert, part of the Kazakh Steppe and part of Ukraine – and completed the final leg in the UK. As the family were based in Atyrau, Kazakhstan between

October 2008 and February 2012, she learnt Russian and was able to help mastermind the Central Asian leg of the ride.

Olga Jaworska

Olga Jaworska (Warsaw, Poland, 1994) lived in Astana, Kazakhstan for three years and recently graduated from the city's QSI International School. Her father works in the Embassy of the Republic of Poland, her mother is an elementary school teacher currently employed at the embassy, and her sister attends eighth grade at QSI. The family has also lived in Russia and as a result Olga speaks fluent Russian. The family has done a lot of travelling in Kazakhstan – to Taraz, Turkestan, Kyzylorda, Karaganda, Balkhash, Pavlodar, Borovoye, Zhezkazgan, Oskemen, Semey and Almaty – as well as to Bishkek and Jalal-Abad in Kyrgyzstan. They are planning a trip to Uzbekistan. Olga fell in love with Kazakhstan and the steppes almost immediately after arriving. "I think the country has made a lot of progress since it achieved independence. This progress is visible even over the three years we have lived here. I would love to share with others the beauty of Central Asia, which is still largely undiscovered." The family has since returned to Poland and Olga will be majoring in Physics at Warsaw University of Technology.

Laura Kennedy

Laura Kennedy (Chicago, Illinois, USA, 1963). She has spent more than 20 years promoting international development and exchange. Laura's interest in all things Soviet first blossomed at Northwestern University, Illinois, USA, where she completed undergraduate work in Russian studies and political science. Laura first travelled to Moscow as a graduate student for four months in 1988, at the height of Perestroika (Mikhail Gorbachev's movement for political reform). While there she had the good luck to work as a production intern for CNN during the Reagan-Gorbachev Summit. This experience sealed her fate as both as 'sovietologist' as well as a news junkie. She went on to spend two summers in the former USSR for work and academic research, before living in Moscow from 1994–1997 while doing doctoral fieldwork on post-Soviet migration. This time she was accompanied by her husband Chris Boffey, an American corporate attorney with a specialty in Russian law.

In 2004, Laura found herself on the move again. The dynamic environment of Central Asia called, bringing Laura, Chris and their two-year old daughter Fiametta to Almaty, Kazakhstan. That same year a second daughter, Amelie, was born. Laura currently works as the Social and Human Sciences Programme Specialist in the Almaty Office of the United Nations Educational, Scientific and Cultural Organization (UNESCO), a position she has held since mid-2005. Her projects in Central Asia focus on labour migration, social inclusion and tolerance issues. In her free time, Laura enjoys volunteering, public speaking and spending time with family and friends, both local and expat, and enjoying the rich cultural mosaic that is Almaty!

Annemarie van Klooster

Annemarie van Klooster (Dordrecht, the Netherlands, 1974) grew up on an inland vessel and attended boarding school during the week from the age of six. When she was 13 years old, she had the opportunity to go to Thailand for six weeks to visit an aunt who had moved there. Annemarie returned home knowing that she wanted to live in Asia one day. When she was

20 years old, she visited her aunt again, this time in Indonesia, with her future husband. After this experience, they both knew they wanted to experience other countries. Today Annemarie is "38 years young" and lives in Kazakhstan with her husband and their three beautiful girls.

Claire McCarthy

Claire McCarthy (Plymouth, England, 1977) is a teacher of Modern Languages and English as Another Language, at the independent school Haileybury Astana. She moved away from her home in the southwest of England to study and has since lived in various cities in the UK, Europe, the Middle East and Central Asia. After graduating as a teacher, she worked as a language teacher in the UK, before moving to Kazakhstan in 2008, to work in Almaty. She then spent a year in the Middle East, before returning to Kazakhstan in 2011, to work in the capital city, Astana.

Laura McLean

During high school and university, Laura McLean (Perth, Canada, 1988) had several opportunities to travel and experience new cultures. Thus, she knew from the outset that she wanted travelling to be a part of her future career. She trained to become an elementary school teacher and took her first official contract in Almaty, Kazakhstan, at an international school. She has been living in Kazakhstan since 2011 and says that every day there has been a learning experience.

Johanna Means

Johanna Means (Punxsutawney, Pennsylvania, USA, 1979) attended Texas A&M University, where she obtained her undergraduate degree in Journalism. After working in social services for a few years, Johanna returned to the University of Pittsburgh to obtain a master's degree in Special Education. She worked in Virginia for four years before deciding to teach internationally. She loves to travel and experience the world. She worked for one year in Astana, Kazakhstan before moving to Shekou, China, where she currently teaches preschool. Johanna would love to see 50 countries by her fiftieth birthday! When she is not working or travelling, she enjoys spending time with friends and cooking.

Antonio Monreale

Antonio Monreale (Parma, Italy, 1963) has lived for more than 20 years in and around Europe and has been in Atyrau since 2008, with his family, wife Carole, and children, Elena (12) and Thomas (6). Although he grew up in Italy, he moved around the country extensively. Thus, when asked, "What part of Italy are you from?", his answer is often, "I don't really know." At the age of 25, Antonio took his first assignment in London, achieving a degree in Computer Science while working. Although his career has been in Information Technology, he has a passion for the humanities and art. He published a book of poetry in 1999, a few essays in a local Italian newspaper in 2009, and a few professional articles in 2010 and 2011. He has a wealth of unpublished creative writing in different forms, which increases with time.

Raquel Taravilla Pujado

Raquel Taravilla Pujado (Barcelona, Spain, 1975) studied Economics at the University of Barcelona. She has 15 years of Human Resources experience behind her, of which 10 years have been in the oil and gas industry. She started her career in HR at a Catalan bank and, six years later, decided to emigrate and extend her horizons. After a six-month sabbatical, she found a job in the Netherlands in an international oil company. Little did she know that this was to be the start of a global career. After almost five years in the Netherlands, she was relocated to Atyrau. Both international postings have given her great knowledge on HR management within a multicultural environment. These days she is working in Italy on another overseas assignment.

Erika Raimondi

Erika Raimondi (Turin, Italy, 1974) is married with three children. Erika went to Atyrau, Kazakhstan, during the summer of 2011, to follow her husband and his work. Since arriving in Kazakhstan she has felt the need to write, to tell of "this world so different and yet so close to us". Her stories are captured in her (Italian) blog, www.mangiaeviaggia.it/blog/erikina. She also contributes to www.expatclic.com, a site that deals with expatriation issues for women.

Alejandra Reyes

Alejandra Reyes (Santiago, Chile, 1970) completed a bachelor of literature at Pontificia Universidad Catolica. After an inspiring experience as an assistant in the exhibition for the Pablo Neruda Foundation in the Museo Nacional Bellas Artes in Santiago, Chile, she decided not to further her literature studies, graduating instead with a degree in Cultural Management of Visual Arts from the Universidad de Chile. Thereafter, she completed an internship in the cultural and journalism department of the Ministry of Foreign Affairs of Chile. Since then, she has been involved in cultural activities in many different countries, such as a collaboration with the Centro Cultural Cervantes for the 'Cultural Month of Latin America' in Cairo, Egypt. Later in Kazakhstan, thanks to the sponsorship of an Italian oil company, she managed two exhibitions for artists whom she continues to represent today. Subsequently, thanks to a different sponsor, she headed an exhibition for the Scottish photographer, Robert Kerr. After a request from a Kazakh human resources company, she managed two other exhibitions showcasing painting, sculpture and photography.

In Italy in November 2011, she produced, with renowned Italian artists such as Clara Brasca, Mario Nava, Silvano Signoreto, Claudio Polles and Luigi Benzoni, an exhibition, sponsored by the Comune di Rho. The prominent art critic Boris Brollo attended this exhibition. More recently, she and Cosimo Mero, professor and managing director of the Antico Oratorio della Passione di Sant'Ambrogio in Milan, have inaugurated a project that aims to establish the woman as a cultural transmitter.

Francesco Le Rose

Francesco Le Rose (Belvedere Marittimo, Italy, 1967) is a management engineer who began his career and his passion for energy sources in the small town of Cetraro in southern Italy. Later, in Rome, he gained work experience as a consultant in an insulation and refrigeration company, before moving to Milan, where he met his wife-to-be and worked at an international oil and gas company. This saw him move to Cairo, where he assumed responsibility in Information Services for north Africa (namely, Egypt, Libya, Algeria and Tunisia) and Iran. He then became involved as CIO in the largest oil and gas industry project in the world in Atyrau, Kazakhstan over the next three years, where he was joined and supported by his wife and two beloved daughters. He now lives in Milan, where he says he is listening to the universe and ready to continue his journey.

Linda van de Sande

Linda van de Sande (Tilburg, the Netherlands, 1986) moved to Belgium to study and attained a Bachelor in Education, majoring in Dutch Language and Art. Thereafter she took some classes to become a certified English as a Foreign Language (EFL) teacher. After her first overseas experience, she became ever more interested in discovering the world. She is passionate about teaching, children, travelling and other cultures. "I like to discover new cultures and to throw myself into cultural experiences," she says. During her stay in Kazakhstan, she learned a lot about the Kazakh culture through local friends. When she's not travelling, you will find her painting, dancing or reading a good book. She hopes her story will inspire readers to visit the vast and interesting land of Kazakhstan.

Tolga Tekiroglu

Tolga Tekiroglu (Ankara, Turkey, 1979) is married to Ozlem, who assisted with writing his story. The couple has two children: daughter Irem (6) and son Erdem (3). Tolga graduated from the Geological Engineering Department at Ankara's Middle East Technical University, before completing an MBA. He started to work in Kazakhstan in 2010, as a country manager for an emergency spill response company, MEKE Kazakhstan. Tolga speaks Turkish (native), English (advanced) and Kazakh (intermediate). His hobbies are oil painting and playing football. He and Ozlem recently moved to Abu Dhabi in the United Arab Emirates.

Machteld Vrieze

Machteld Vrieze (Deventer, the Netherlands, 1976) has lived in Curacao, Dutch Antilles (1980–1984) and Paris, France (2002–2003). She trained as a lawyer specialising in public and environmental law. In Kazakhstan, where she has lived since 2010, she is mother to three boys and a part-time legal auditor, though she also describes herself as "an idealist, a writer and a singer". She is married to a Dutchman, who is the director of the Witteveen+Bos branch in Atyrau, Kazakhstan. She spends her free time enjoying her family, as well as the countless peculiarities of the Kazakh culture and the ingenuity of its expats. She has already attended six Kazakh weddings – it was these experiences that inspired her story – and two more are expected this year. Find her blog about Kazakhstan at http://machinkaz.blogsnel.nl.

BITTEN BY SPAIN

THE MURCIAN COUNTRYSIDE
– A BAPTISM BY FIRE

DEBORAH FLETCHER

... had me chuckling from the first page till the last"
Vanessa Rocchetta, Expatica.com

"An entertaining story,
told with wit and insight"
Paul Burston, author, The Gay Divorcee

PERKING
THE PANSIES

*Jack and Liam
move to Turkey*

JACK SCOTT

FLY AWAY
HOME

Maggie Myklebust

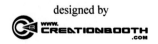

Lightning Source UK Ltd.
Milton Keynes UK
UKOW02f1606141215

264698UK00002B/32/P